MW01517923

A Father's Tears

A Father's Tears

No part of this book may be reproduced, stored in a retrieval system or transmitted in any form or by any means, electronic, mechanical, photocopying, recording, scanning or otherwise, except as permitted by law, without the prior written permission of the author.

The writing provided in this book is designed to provide helpful information on the subjects discussed. This book is not meant to be used nor should it be used, to diagnose or treat any medical condition. For diagnosis or treatment of any medical problem, consult your own physician. The publisher and author are not responsible for any specific health needs that may require medical supervision and are not liable for any damages or negative consequences from any treatment, action, application or preparation, to any person reading or following the information in this book. References are provided for informational purposes only and do not constitute endorsement of any websites or other sources. Readers should be aware that the websites listed in this book may change.

This book is designed to provide information to readers. It is sold with the understanding that the author and publisher are not engaged to render any type of psychological, legal, or any other kind of professional advice. The content of this book is the sole expression and opinion of its author, and not necessarily that of the publisher. No warranties or guarantees are expressed or implied by the publisher's choice to include any of the content in this volume. Neither the publisher nor the author shall be liable for any physical, psychological, emotional, financial, or commercial damages, including, but not limited to, special, incidental, consequential or other damages. Our views and rights are the same: You are responsible for your own choices, actions, and results.

The names of some of the people in this book have been changed out of respect for their privacy.

Copyright © 2012; David McColl

Cover photo by: Charlotte Boiral

Cover design by: David McColl

Edited by: Sheryl Bennett-Wilson

All rights reserved.

Table of Contents

Dedication

This book is dedicated to all of the people of the community of Aylmer, Quebec. The support we continue to receive from all of you is truly humbling and we wouldn't have been able to deal with this tragedy as well as we have without you. "A Father's Tears" is also dedicated to all of the people whom we don't know but have offered kind and loving support to my family and the Tony's Promise campaign;

http://www.tonyspromise.org/

A huge thanks to all of the people on the Tony's Promise Face Book group;

http://www.facebook.com/groups/tonyspromise/

By consistently spreading the Promise, you are saving people's lives and making the world a better and safer place. I also dedicate this book to the kind people who have taken a part of my son with them on their travels around the world. Tony's Traveling Ashes is a way of keeping my son's name alive.

Acknowledgements

My journey through grief has been shared with a great number of people. If it weren't for Sheryl Bennett-Wilson, Laurie Wilson and Lynn Tarzwell, I wouldn't have written one word about this painful journey. People like, Rick and Peggy Henderson, Andy Wilson, John Tarzwell, my beautiful sister, Joanne Van Doorn and all of the kind people who have taken my son's ashes to the far corners of the planet. All of the community of Aylmer, Quebec for their kind support. Everyone who brought all of that food, especially the lasagna.

I want to thank Mr. Martin Crosbie, the author of "My Temporary Life". I read about him in The Globe and Mail and after contacting him, he immediately offered to help and took me by the hand and lead me down the path of self-publishing, without hesitation.

I want to thank the "Fantastic Four", Richard Beard, Andy Guest, Parker Johnston and Luc Leblanc for creating "Tony's Promise" and helping save lives in my son's name.

Most of all I want to thank my beauties, my wife Monica and my daughter Alanna. Both of you have been so understanding and supportive. Where some families would have been torn apart by this tragedy, you chose to work together as a family and shared your pain and thoughts openly with me. Alanna, knowing how much you loved your big brother, you show such incredible strength and maturity in dealing with the loss and the guilt. I love you both so much.

Why I wrote this Book

I have a number of close friends that write for a living. One teaches script writing, another writes marketing material and a third writes press releases and various media documents. Shortly after the accident all three of them mentioned that it may be cathartic if I kept a journal of my thoughts and feelings. I have struggled with writing all my life. I was overcome with grief and naturally reluctant to start writing about anything at this point.

But my friends persisted. They bought me a journal to keep with me and document my thoughts at any particular moment. I thanked them, put the journal away and haven't seen it since that day. Finally in February 2012, my writer friend Laurie called to chat. After about twenty minutes she said, "You really should consider writing a book about this experience".
Well, that was the last straw.
"Okay, I'll write something", thinking, "Just to stop these people from asking me to write".
And that was the beginning of what you are now reading.

After all of this encouragement, I decided to write this book for four reasons.

The first was that perhaps it would be a cathartic experience-although I was convinced that I had been going through catharsis each time I spoke of my son and the circumstances related to his death. Having said that, I have to admit that writing this has definitely helped me. Each and every time I worked on this book I shed tears.

The second reason was that I don't want my son's name to be forgotten. In the case of the all too common tragic road accident due to reasons that were completely preventable, names are mentioned and people say, "who"?

This comment is usually followed by, "oh yes, I think I remember that story, the kid out in some back road crash, it was late at night", etc.... This is also a sign of the abundance of tragic road accidents.

The third reason for writing this book is that men have a very difficult time dealing with grief. Our culture dictates that men are not to show grief, it's a sign of weakness. Well, men are affected by grief. We are not immune to the effects of the power of grief. We are capable of crying and we do cry. Men are expected to handle it. "Man up", as it were. This is very apparent in times of war. Soldiers witness unimaginable horror. Scenes that affect them for the rest of their lives, but they're expected to suck it up and get over it. We have seen the effects of veterans "sucking it up" and it simply doesn't work.

Suicides due to Post Traumatic Stress Disorder (PTSD) are covered up and reported as resulting from substance abuse or a cause that the military refuses to deal with. This is not new. PTSD has occurred since wars began.

The fourth reason for writing this book is that my research shows that women write most books related to dealing with grief. Those that are written by men are usually written by male psychiatrists and psychologists. Very few "ordinary", nonprofessional men write about the grief that they are suffering or have suffered.

All of these reasons lead mainly to the hope that by my writing about my personal experience with grief, I may assist men and women in dealing with their own, personal struggles with grief.

I also speak to schools, parent groups and various organizations about making the right decisions when it comes to driving. I speak about the Tony's Promise campaign and dealing with the death of a child. If you would

like me to speak on these topics, I may be contacted by email
at;

mccoll@videotron.ca

Or

David McColl
c/o Tony's Promise
181 rue Principale
P.O. Box 76064
Gatineau, Quebec
Canada
J9H 6W0

I was also encouraged to write this book because a number of
people (all women), the majority of whom I had never met
contacted me. They had either seen my son's story in the
media or through the Tony's Promise Face Book group and
were going through the same terrible struggle that my family
and I are going through.

I'd get messages saying, "It is my first Mother's Day since my
son died in a car crash, how do I get through it"?
Or
"My ex-husband and my step son were killed in a car accident
and my children are having difficulty dealing with the loss.
Can you please speak to them and help them get through it"?

A big part of this book is about making decisions.

Unconscious decisions. We make them all of the time and usually we get by okay. As you read you will see how a few decisions were made nonchalantly. These decisions resulted in two deaths. It's important to think about the things you do, especially when driving. The decision to drive while under the influence of drugs or alcohol. The decision to wear a seat belt or not. Most importantly the decision of what to do when you are about to be pulled over by a police car. All three of these decisions are made regularly and making the wrong decision can end in a very bad way. Remember, the choice is always yours to make.

If you are going through the unbearable experience of losing a child, know that you are not alone. Too many people lose children.
I hope my writing helps.

The Call

I awoke at 6:00 AM to the sound of my wife's cell phone ringing. Who would be calling Monica's cell at this hour, I thought? We had left home just 12 hours before to have dinner at a friend's cottage. We'd spend the night and were going to return home after breakfast.

While Monica went to retrieve her phone in another room, I thought to myself, her number ends in 9999, it was probably someone misdialing. That happens regularly.

I heard my wife say, "Alanna, what's wrong sweetie?" She handed the phone to me. It was our daughter Alanna, crying and hysterical. "Anthony's been in a serious accident, get to the Hull hospital as soon as you can!"

"OK, sweetie, calm down, what happened", I said. She was still crying but comforted by my voice, she responded, "I don't know except he's been in a serious accident and the police need to see you as soon as possible. I'm at the hospital and they won't tell me anything. Please hurry."

"Are you alone", I asked. "No", she said, "Rebecca and her family are here, just get here."

"OK, sweetie, but it'll take us an hour to get to you because we're at Linda's cottage. We'll get there as soon as we can", I said, with a churning feeling starting in my stomach. Our son had turned nineteen five weeks earlier. He's a big and powerful man standing 6 feet 4 inches tall and weighing in at 230 pounds. He was a formidable rugby player, a musician and a loving, protective brother to his sister Alanna. What could have happened?

Alanna had been at a birthday party for a friend the night before. The friend lived on a farm about 40 minutes outside of town. Earlier Friday evening Anthony had used his mother's 2008 Honda Civic for his pizza delivery job at a local restaurant. He had a regular shift every Friday. After he finished work at 8:00 he was to check with Alanna. He'd go to the party and pick her up, but only if she needed a ride. If not, he'd leave the car at home and head out to meet up with friends on foot or by bus.

We quickly threw our things together and went out to the car. It was Saturday, April 16, 2011. The sky was overcast and nothing was budding yet. None of the flora had started its annual growth. The beautiful beginnings of spring, vivid greens of new foliage sprouting from tree branches had yet to start. It was just a cloudy, cool and dull grey day.

As Monica and I started the drive I set the cruise control to the exact speed limit. I didn't want to inadvertently drive too quickly and risk having my own accident, or draw the attention of the police. I was determined to ensure a safe trip to the hospital while pondering how "serious" Anthony's accident was.

Monica spoke first.
"Maybe he got hit by a car while long boarding", she said.
I could hear the expected tone of worry in a mother's voice. My thoughts were of arriving at the hospital to see my son with casts on at least a leg or an arm or both. Anthony was a good and conscientious driver and I knew that whatever happened it wouldn't have been his fault.

I continued driving and constantly checked my speed as if I mistrusted the cruise control. I wanted to get there, but I needed to get there safely.

It was a long drive. Only one hour, but running all of the possible scenarios through my head made it seem like an eternity.

I pondered a broken bones scenario possibly caused by a long boarding accident. Suddenly a vision of my son connected to a multitude of machines and in a coma flashed through my mind. No, not my Anthony. He was too good for that. We were too good for that to happen to us. Death? I don't recall the thought of my son dying entering my mind during the long drive to the hospital.

I do remember something about that drive that I recalled after leaving the hospital some two hours later. If anyone drives in rural areas of North America, it's not uncommon to see numerous roadside memorials for people that have died in car accidents. I've noticed many of them over the years. Hastily constructed crosses with "R.I.P." and the nickname of the deceased, surrounded by an assortment of mementoes, flowers and teddy bears honoring the victim or victims. I would often think about who had died here. Who was it? Who did they leave behind? I also used to think to myself, I live in a community of about 60,000 people. Someone we all know is going to have their own little road side grotto as a result of a crash, but who and when? Will it be one of the kids we know that has a penchant for getting into mischief? Some kid new to driving, getting in over his head going through a corner? Well, it won't be us. We're good people, our kids do well in school. They don't take drugs. Monica and I have worked very hard to teach Anthony and Alanna the right way to live. Get involved in the community, be good at school and be polite, etc. And it worked. They are model kids and people tell us so. We don't deserve a sad and pathetic roadside memorial, those are for other people.

In the past I remember distinctly thinking as I drove by the far too many memorials, "some poor teenager either killed himself or someone driving erratically killed him, poor bastard."

Another thing that came to mind a few days later was how everything around us during that drive to the hospital was grey and dull. No color, spring still a few weeks away. One thing did stand out though. As we drove to the hospital, I recall counting four of those sad roadside memorials. I also recalled that at each of those memorials (it appeared that) someone had left fresh flowers. I remember now noticing how vivid the color of the flowers were at each memorial and thinking, "wow, someone is really taking care of these sacred places."

In the weeks that followed those flowers would haunt me. The prophecy of what was to come.

We arrived at the hospital. I dropped Monica at the main entrance so one of us could get to Alanna as soon as possible. The hospital had recently undergone a major renovation so the main entrance was now at the furthest possible point from the Emergency area.

After following the yellow lines on the floor for what seemed another hour, I caught up with my wife. We finally got to Emergency. The waiting area was large and impressive. I remembered the old waiting area. I'd visited it many years earlier. A neighbor of ours had a sudden kidney stone attack at 5:00 AM, I'd followed the ambulance and dropped his wife Samantha off at the hospital. I'll never forget that visit. I waited beside Samantha while she gave the receptionist her husband's name and information at the administration desk. Immediately next to the desk was a display of what looked like greeting cards. I took a closer look. They were bereavement cards. Cards that had "Condolences for your loss" and "With deepest sympathies" printed on them. I will never forget that visit.

After identifying ourselves to the receptionist, we were escorted to a small room just off of the main waiting area. It didn't occur to me at the time but I found that odd as well. Why weren't we led to the "normal" waiting area? When we entered the small room Alanna rushed into my arms crying. Instead of asking questions all I could do was console her.

Rebecca, Alanna's best friend was also there with her parents. I then noticed that there were at least four other adults sitting there, who I didn't know. Wanting to get more information I asked openly, "does anyone know what happened?" Someone said that there'd been a bad car accident and that their daughter was in the car. Things went somewhat blurry at that point. I remember speaking to someone, man or woman, I don't know. Someone said that Anthony had been driving his car and it had crashed. I looked over at an older man wearing a baseball hat, sitting in a wheelchair off to the side and asked, "Was your daughter in the car too"?

He replied, "No, my son was in the other car".

"Is he OK", I asked?

He replied, "I don't know, but it doesn't look good".

His voice whimpered as he held back tears.

What was I hearing? There'd been an accident involving two cars, one with my son and at least one girl in it. The second car had someone else's son it? And "it doesn't look good"? The churning in my stomach was starting to become more intense.

I looked at one of the other couples in the room, "who are you"?

"We're Chelsea's parents".

Who is Chelsea?

Alanna said, "Chelsea, Lea, Kayla and Alexa were in the car with Anthony". What? Were there four girls in the car with my son when it had an accident? "Are they OK", I blurted out. Someone said, "They are in serious condition, Lea is in critical condition and that's all we know".

Good Lord, what's going on here? This doesn't happen to good people like us. I was getting confused. Why hadn't I been able to see my son yet? I walked out to the reception area. "When can I see my son", I demanded. "The doctors are very busy treating all of the patients and will be with you as soon as possible", said the receptionist. She had a sad, painful look on her face. I wandered back into the small waiting room and approached the man in the wheel chair. I reached out my hand and introduced myself. When I shook his hand I could see his bent, arthritic fingers. "I'm John Campbell and this is my wife Bev", he replied. "My son Brian was driving the other car. He works in the east end of Ottawa at an auto repair shop and was on his way home for the weekend".

"Was anyone in the car with him", I asked?

"No", replied John.

"Do you know what happened"? Hoping to get any scrap of information.

"No, just that there was a bad accident", he said with his head bowed, looking at the floor.

"Are you from Aylmer"?

"We have a farm in Shawville," he answered.

Shawville is about 40 minutes west of Aylmer, Quebec, and a farming community on the infamous Highway 148.

There have been numerous deadly accidents on the 148 over the years. Sixteen deaths in 2011, 12 of which were preventable, according to local police. If you drive along highway 148 you're reminded of these far too frequent accidents by the constant site of roadside memorials erected by friends and family of the victims.

One of the most bizarre accidents on highway 148 occurred a month and a half after my son's accident and exactly 1 kilometer west. A westbound car travelling at approximately 90 kilometers an hour hit a large bear that ran onto the highway. The bear was vaulted high into the air by the impact. On its decent it hit the driver's side windshield of a vehicle traveling in the opposite direction. The impact was devastating. The bear passed through the windshield, killing

---

the driver instantly and seriously injuring the front passenger. It didn't end there. The body of the bear continued its trajectory through the car. The impact killed the passenger sitting directly behind the driver, before smashing through the back window of the car. The bear ended up a torn and bloody mess on the side of the highway. Obviously it died on impact. Coincidentally, the passenger who was killed sitting in the back of the car had a son that played football with my son in grade 7.

A nurse enters the waiting area and speaks to the members of one of the other families. She asks them to follow her. What's going on with Anthony, why aren't we getting any information, and why can't we see him, I wonder? My thoughts quickly flash again to him, laying on a gurney with tubes in his mouth and intravenous lines taped to his arms. His eyes are closed and his body connected to countless monitoring devices that are beeping. In my vision he is surrounded by a blur of medical personnel rushing around, stepping over scattered bits of discarded medical device wrappers and scraps of cloth and tape.

The nurse enters the room again and requests the Campbell family to follow her. Mrs. Campbell wheels John out of the waiting room. We sit there, waiting and wondering. How bad can it be? What does it mean to be asked last in an accident that involved serious injuries with multiple victims?

Alanna asks if she can go outside and get some air with her friend. I agree but ask that she not wander off too far. The nurse comes back. They're ready for us. But where is Alanna? We send someone off to find her.

As we exit the waiting room a man and woman enter.
"Are you the father of one of the girls"? I ask.
He said a girl's name but it didn't register.
"Are you Tony's father"?
"Yes", I responded.
"I'm sorry for your loss", he said.
"What"?! I said in surprise.
"Did you see him"?

Sorry for your loss? What does that mean, I thought to myself? We continued to follow the nurse through a large heavy door with a sign on it that said "Hospital Staff Only". I was finally going to see my son.

Immediately after passing through the large door, there was another door to the left. The door was slightly open. I could clearly see two gurneys with what appeared to be bodies on them. I assumed that they were bodies because whatever was on them was draped with those typical yellow plastic sheets that Paramedics use, similar to the ones you see on the news. There was a woman in the room. She was about 35 years old and wearing glasses. She was writing something on a clipboard. I assumed she was not medical staff, as she wasn't wearing any medical-type clothing. She looked up at me and went back to her writing. I thought for a fleeting moment that this may be part of the Intensive Care unit. But that thought was quickly dismissed by the absence of the sight or sound of any life saving equipment. It was just a quiet room with a young, serious looking woman making notes. My eyes moved to the sign on the door, "Pathology" was all it said. Pathology. Isn't that a type of medical jargon? "Get these samples down to the Pathology lab", people say in movies and on television. My stomach was alerting me again that something was wrong. I started to feel a little weak in the knees.

We entered a small office around the corner from the Pathology room with the nurse. A doctor who looked like he had been working for a week nonstop was in the office. Where is Alanna, she should be here? The nurse offered to go and find her. She returned a few moments later and told us that she'd directed a police officer to go outside and bring her to us. The nurse sat down and held Monica's hand as the doctor introduced himself. "I'm Dr. Smith, I was the attending physician on last night's shift when the ambulance arrived".

"I've been tending to the girls and they've been injured very seriously", he continued.

"There was a very bad car accident between your son's car and another vehicle at approximately 2:30 this morning in Luskville on highway 148".

For God's sake what is going on here, I want to see my son, I screamed inside my head. The nurse was looking at Monica, with a pained look on her face. She was nodding her head, as if to say "you know what he is about to tell you".

The doctor seemed very reluctant to speak about Anthony, to a point where I was about to grab him by the lapels and say, "please just tell us what condition he is in"! He continued, "the accident involved a police chase, the two cars collided and, your son... is dead".

Monica started to cry and wail "no, no, no... Oh my God"! The nurse held Monica's hand and tried, in vain to console her. I sat there looking at what was going on around me as if I were watching it on television. My wife screaming. A very tired looking Doctor clearly not used to telling parents that their first-born had been killed in a violent car accident. An experienced and hardened looking nurse who had obviously been in this same position many times. My own feelings surprised me. I showed no emotion and I knew it. I pictured myself sitting there, stunned. What was I supposed to do? Was I to scream as well? What does the father do at this point? I had no previous experience or references to deal with the news. I did nothing. I sat there in shock and I knew I was in shock. As I heard the screaming and noise around me, I remember feeling somewhat nervous. Why on earth would I feel nervous, I thought? I still can't explain my feelings and lack of reaction at that moment.

Then Alanna walked in the door. "What happened", she asked. Monica looked at her and said, "you know... I think you know... Anthony is dead".

Alanna started to cry as the doctor looked at Monica and me and said, "you may see him now, if you wish". The nurse added quickly, looking at Alanna, "I don't think you should go in there, it's pretty bad".

"I don't think you should see him, it's not a nice thing to look at", she added.

"No", Alanna shouted through heavy tears, "I want to see my brother"!

The nurse replied, "OK", but you must be prepared for what you see".

"I don't care, I want to see my brother", she insisted.

We got up and the nurse led us to the Pathology room, the one I'd noticed earlier. So that is my son under that yellow plastic, death sheet I thought. I realized that as we'd passed the pathology room initially, I knew it was my Anthony on one of those gurneys. But I simply couldn't accept it.

As we entered the room, I was struck by how small it was. The two gurneys barely fit. What will he look like, I thought? The nurse once again tried to prepare us for what we were about to see. The nurse was in front, followed by Alanna and Monica. I was at the end of the line. The nurse peeled back the yellow sheet to expose my son from the chest up. He lay there looking grey; his head turned slightly to his right. The hair that I admired so much throughout his short life had been cut a few weeks prior and was a little messy. His eyes were slightly open and looking unfocused over my left shoulder, exactly as they used to when he was a baby, deep in sleep. I tried to close his eyes just as I used to while checking on him before I turned in for the night. This made me think of the movies when someone closes the eyes of a dead character. But this was reality, not a movie and his eyes refused to close. So much for movies, I thought. Two separate streams of blood trickled down his face. One from his right nostril and the other from the right corner of his mouth. The nurse wiped them away as if knowing that was where I was looking. Suddenly I was jolted out of my thoughts by the screams of Monica. "My baby boy, my beautiful baby boy, why, why, I love you, I love you, I love you"! Monica's keening screams were so loud and painful that even the hardened emergency room staff seemed to wince at the sound. I was told many months later that the girls involved in the accident that still remained in the emergency room were kept awake at night for months by the memory of those painful, howling screams that morning.

I recalled that almost immediately after the nurse peeled back the sheet, Alanna shouted something I didn't understand and she ran from the room crying. I knew she'd lost her brother, protector and confidante, but I couldn't be with her. I had to stay. I had to be with my boy.

He was wearing his favorite shirt, a red sleeveless basketball style shirt with a skateboard logo on it. I held his cold hand. It still felt large and powerful, my six foot four two hundred and thirty pound rugby-playing son, I stroked his short hair, thinking that just weeks prior, he had long, flowing, wavy hair that he intended to convert into dreadlocks, much to my chagrin.

About 2 weeks earlier he'd come into the kitchen and said "Dad, do you mind if cut my hair, it's driving me crazy"?
"No dreads"?, I replied trying to hide my pleasure.
"No, it's too long and it's really bothering me".
"How short are you going to cut it", I asked, praying he wouldn't say; "bean shave".
"Just a trim, I want to keep it out of my eyes".
"Sure", I responded casually, while inside I was doing cart wheels, "but go upstairs right now, wash it, blow dry it and come back so I can take some photos of you before you cut it".

I'm a serious, semi-professional photojournalist. It's one of my hobbies. I've taken thousands of photos of both Anthony and Alanna playing sports, traveling together virtually-anything I could shoot with them in it. I've had a number of shots of both Anthony and Alanna playing sports published in local newspapers and was very proud to show them off.

Anthony did as I asked, came down stairs and I clicked away. They were the last photographs I took of my son. It's funny the things that go through your mind at times like this.

As I stood beside my son's lifeless body, I realized I smelled something. It was a curious combination of things. My son's unique and pleasant personal scent, combined with the smell of his sweat and a hint of what I can only imagine was the smell of blood and fecal matter. Another rather surprising thing came to mind as I stared down at his grey motionless body. If he was killed in a violent car accident, apparently a head-on collision, why does he look so good? I mean, he certainly looked dead, but I distinctly remember thinking, "he doesn't look that bad for a person who has been in a violent automobile accident"! In fact he didn't look that bad in death. Prior to that day, I would have imagined that like all of us in old age he would look far worse on his deathbed.

The driver of the other vehicle was not so lucky. Apparently he wasn't wearing his seat belt and was ejected from the car through a closed window. His body ended up thirty or forty feet down the road. Although he was on the gurney next to Anthony and although I could have done so, I didn't have the inclination to pull down the sheet to look at him. It must have been a very graphic and traumatizing sight for his parents.

Many months later the first responders to the accident from the Luskville Fire Department held a fund raising barbeque in Anthony's honor. During this event I had detailed conversations with these great people and I made an interesting discovery. The leader of the fire department team there that night expressed his surprise at how "clean" Anthony was in terms of visible trauma. I can only thank God that he was so "clean".

I was in a daze the whole time. I felt nothing. I imagine I was in extreme shock. I felt numb with little sadness or pain. I was in a major state of stunned disbelief. For some reason I left the pathology room, I guess it was instinct to go and see how Alanna was doing. Monica remained. She was talking to Anthony but I couldn't make out her tear-filled words.

The next thing I remember was being led back to the doctor's office. We had to sign a number of documents, death certificate maybe. I have no idea. It was all a blur.

We finally ended up back in the small waiting room. If anyone else was in the room, I don't recall. I simply remember sobbing. My face was buried in my hands. My shoulders heaved with sobs of the most profound sadness I'd ever experienced. I remember being startled at the sound of my own crying; suddenly hoping I was alone so no one could see the weakness I was showing. Weakness. I love my son, and to cry upon seeing him dead is considered a weakness in men? How dare I feel guilty for crying over my dead son. How dare our culture suggest that a crying man is weak. My son is worth every sob, every stinging tear that pours from my eyes. I refuse to feel "weak" because I cry over my son's death. The hell with male cultural machismo and to hell with anyone who dares to challenge me on that.

"Now I know there is no God", I muttered to no one in particular in the waiting room.
"Pardon", my wife said?
"Now I know there is no fucking God"! I blasted, perhaps with too much volume and anger.
Why would God do this to my family?

I felt a hand on my shoulder, a comforting hand. I guess I wasn't alone. I assumed it was my wife's hand but found out some nine months later that it had been Alanna's hand. My darling Alanna offering me comfort. It is both uplifting and embarrassing to know that she saw me in such a pathetic state. There's that Goddamned machismo thing again. As Alanna explained so many months later, it had indeed been her hand on my shoulder. She also mentioned at how surprised and disturbed she was at seeing me cry. I suppose that prior to this moment I was always the rock. I was the guy that never got emotional. I was always steadfast and stalwart in difficult times. I remember on a number of occasions prior to Anthony's death Alanna would ask, "dad how come you never cry, I want to see you cry"?

"I'll cry at your wedding", was my usual response. Those will be tears of joy. Not tears generated by utter, debilitating sadness.

As I pulled my self back to reality I realized that the parents of Alanna's friend Rebecca were in the room with Monica and Alanna. They'd seen me unravel and heard my harsh words. Even in my bereft, emotional state, I hoped they weren't religious and didn't take offence.

A few moments later the woman that we'd seen in the Pathology room entered and introduced herself to us. She was the local police Sergeant in charge of the investigation. She proceeded to give us the details of the accident from the notes on her clipboard. The following is what I recall her telling us;

At approximately 2:30 AM on Saturday, April 16, a car heading west on highway 148 caught the attention of a parked police cruiser. The officers in the car decided to do a routine check and began to follow the passing car. The driver of the car noticed the police vehicle and began to accelerate. The police now accelerated as well and at some point turned on their police lights. The driver of the vehicle increased his speed and began to pass vehicles. It became a police chase. After recording the suspect vehicle's license number, the police decided to stop the pursuit. The speed of the evading car was climbing to a dangerous level. In hopes that the errant driver would slow down, "the police car reduced speed and followed at a distance". Moments later, the suspect car veered onto the shoulder of the road and in correcting the move, crossed the centerline of the highway and into the path of Anthony's car. The driver of the pursued vehicle was ejected from his car and died instantly.

I don't remember if the Sergeant told us when Anthony died but I do know the newspaper reported that he died some hours after the accident. Dear Lord, please make that not true, I thought. I saw him in the hospital. He looked as if he died peacefully. I've read many books on WWI and the Vietnam War. There are numerous accounts of soldiers dying with an expression of pain frozen on their faces. One of our worries was whether Anthony suffered or not. We couldn't live with the knowledge that our baby boy suffered a painful death.

The Sergeant continued;

There were four girls in the car. Alanna was supposed to be one of them. All four girls were seriously injured. Two were in critical condition. Lea, who was sitting in front, next to Anthony, was in the most serious condition as far as they could tell. She had a fractured pelvis, a broken leg, a broken wrist and a bad gash on her forehead over her left eye. Lea was later taken to a hospital in Montreal for one of two surgeries to repair her shattered pelvic bone. In the weeks that followed, the question of her ever being able to walk again came up, as well as the possibility of her losing her left eye.

Alexa, who was sitting behind Lea, suffered a broken collarbone.

It turns out that Alexa suffered the least number of injuries, at least physically. Kayla was sitting in the middle of the back seat. She'd suffered from cancer in her right knee a number of years earlier. Her cancerous knee had been replaced with a prosthetic implant at the time. The impact of the crash was so hard that the prosthetic shattered her femur. Kayla was rushed to the Children's Hospital of Eastern Ontario and remained in hospital for many months.

Chelsea sat directly behind Anthony. She suffered a broken collarbone and broken humerus. The humerus is the bone between your shoulder and your elbow and is the third largest bone in your body. "Will they be alright", I asked the Sergeant?

"I don't know for sure", she replied.

"Your son died of lower extremity and internal injuries", she continued.

"You'll get the results of the autopsy when it is completed", she added.

"What were the circumstances of the accident", I asked?

"Due to the fact that is was a police chase and deaths were involved, the investigation will be handed over to the Quebec Provincial Police", was her response.

"They'll be contacting you. In the meantime, if you have any more questions, here's my card", she handed me a card. I stuffed it in my pocket.

"Here are some of his personal effects".

She handed me a plastic zip lock bag.

In it was the necklace we bought for Anthony in Toronto the previous Christmas. It was a black stone that's common on the beaches of New Zealand. The stone had an ornate pattern carved into it and is on a leather string. No gold chains for Anthony, too flashy. He loved that stone and wore it everywhere. I took it out of the bag. What got my attention was how it smelled. The smell wasn't Anthony's usual pleasant "personal" aroma. It was simply sweat and blood. I concluded this was my son's "death smell". I didn't like it.

The Sergeant said a few more things that I immediately forgot and we said thank you. What's next? What do we do now? I can recall little of the time between then and getting into my car. I imagine the nurse or the Sergeant suggested it was time to go. As we left the hospital, Rebecca's father Gerry, asked if we would like him to drive us home.

"No thank you, I replied, "we'll be OK".

"Are you sure? I could drive you in your car and my wife could follow in our car", he offered.

"No thanks Gerry, I made it here from the cottage. I'll be extra careful, thanks anyway", I asserted.

"OK. But I'll follow you and make sure you get home alright", he concluded.

"Thanks Gerry, that would be great, and thank you so much for being here with Alanna while we drove in from the country", somehow I remembered to say these things. God knows how?

We wandered to the car. The morning was cool, grey and still. I felt a shiver as it started to lightly rain. We were leaving the hospital. My son was to remain there, dead. On a gurney. Smelling of death and bleeding from his nose and mouth. What would they do to him in the hospital? Indeed, what unimaginable things would they do to that perfect, powerful body? What about his organs? He was young and strong. Could his organs not be used to help someone else? I felt pangs of guilt for not asking the hospital about donating his organs. Then I remembered...

"The cause of death was lower extremity and internal organ damage". That forced me to think that perhaps none of his organs were in any condition to be given to anyone. My God,

my poor boy, I hope he didn't suffer. Please, someone tell me he didn't suffer. I couldn't bear the thought of it and put it out of my mind. Now we had to get home safely.

We got into the car. I started the car and sat for a moment with my wife and daughter.

Something in my head said that I had to make sure that we don't fall apart. I've got to make sure we stick together through this tragedy. I don't know what gave me this moment of clarity. Perhaps it was a flash of the remains of my family coming apart. Making a bad situation worse, but I had to tell them.

"This is a terrible thing that has happened to us", I started. "And we have to make sure of three things. We have to make sure we eat properly, because there will be times when we won't want to eat. We must get the proper amount of sleep. And most of all we have to make sure we get along with each other". I said with a lump in my throat.

"I don't want to be an only child"! Alanna shouted in tears. "I don't want to be an only child"!

I shifted into drive and we headed home.

The Onslaught

We arrived home with Gerry in tow. He got out of the car and said if there was anything we needed, simply to call. I thanked him again. I didn't know it at the time but we'd be hearing those words a lot in the weeks to come.

We entered the house and the first thing I did was rummage through the pantry looking for something for us to eat. I was determined to try to keep my remaining family members healthy for what was sure to be an emotionally trying time. I found a rather dated package of chicken noodle soup. The soup was the powdered kind. You just add water and boil it. It probably contains no chicken whatsoever and has those short, skinny noodles. At least it was something to put in our stomachs.

How appropriate, chicken soup is supposed to cure everything, I thought. It's going to take a lot of soup to cure our ills.

I put the soup into a pot, added water, boiled it and served a small amount to Monica and Alanna.

"Make sure you eat some of this, we need to look after ourselves or we'll get sick and we don't need that right now".

Even though I had absolutely no appetite, I forced myself to drink a few sips of the salty mixture. Monica and Alanna sat there staring at the soup in front of them on the table.

"I'm not hungry", Alanna said.

"Have a few mouths full anyway, the next few days will be very busy and we must eat, even if we don't feel like it". I responded.

Monica said nothing, and, like a robot programmed to eat, she picked up her spoon and ate the soup in silence.

What do we do now, I thought to myself. I have no prior experience with anything like this. When my parents died, I was somewhat prepared. They were old and sick. My sister and I made the arrangements for them and all went as it should. I'd anticipated my parent's dying. They hadn't been well for a while, it was their "time" and I could accept that. So I took things in stride. But that in no way prepared me for the death of my 19-year-old son. Is anyone ever prepared for the death of his or her child?

How was it that everyone seemed to know Anthony was dead before we did? The father of one of the girls in the hospital knew. Did his daughter tell him? I quickly thought that word must have traveled through social media and the news.

The news! Turn on the news. We turned on the radio and there it was. There were broadcasts on every station imaginable about the tragic death of a loved brother, son and friend.

"We should see if it's in the newspaper. I'll walk up to the store and buy one, I'll be back in 10 minutes", I said to Monica.

I put on my work boots because it was raining out and proceeded to the corner store. Walking slowly in the rain, I felt the beginnings of what I would later call the anvil in my chest. An anvil is the only way to describe it. It felt as if there had been an anvil implanted in my chest with wires attached to each of my shoulders. The weight of it made me slump as I walked along the street. It was a blustery day. That only added to my sadness. But I was yet to feel the true weight of sadness and grief. At this point I was in shock. What I was feeling was nothing compared to how heavy the anvil would get.

I entered the store and picked up a copy of The Ottawa Sun. There it was on the front page. The headline simply said "Tragic", followed by "Protective big brother killed in head-on collision by suspected drunk driver fleeing cops". There was a picture of my Anto. It was a photo I had taken for a project he was doing for his visual arts program at school. In the shot he is smiling. His hair is long and curly. His beautiful hair I adored so much. There was also a photo of the car, or what was left of it. I assumed the police took the photo. It was taken in daylight and it was shocking.

The car was absolutely destroyed. The first responders had to use the Jaws of Life to extricate the passengers. The roof was completely gone. Clearly cut off, it wasn't even visible in the photograph. There were large pieces of debris on the road as well as countless bits of metal and plastic scattered everywhere. It must have been a devastating impact. How could anyone have survived a crash of this severity, I thought. It was almost unbelievable. I took two copies and went to the cash. George, the storeowner is a well-known local character. He never seems to be away from the place. Anthony used to speak of him often. "I went to the store the other day and saw gruff old George", Anthony would say, chuckling.

"Hi George", Anthony would say and George's usual response was more of a grunt than a greeting. George was always pleasant in his gruffness. I showed George the front page of the paper and said, "Do you recognize this kid"?

"Yep".

"That's my son", I said, choking back tears.

"I blame the fucking cops for that", George added, to my surprise.

I thanked him and left the store.

On my way home it was raining a little harder. There's no sidewalk on the side of the street I was walking on, only puddles. The water was following its gravitational path to sewer drains. I had a sudden flash of memory. When Anthony was a little boy we would sometimes go for walks just after it had rained. He'd wear his rubber boots and take great joy in walking through the puddles, splashing and kicking the water. Remembering that, I started to walk through the puddles, gently moving the water along its path and brushing away the mini dams created by gathering leaves. My eyes filled with tears as I walked the rest of the way home through the puddles.

What went through his mind during those last minutes of life, I wondered. How did it feel? Dear God I hope he didn't suffer. I also wondered how his passengers were doing and hoped that they would be OK.

I arrived home and showed the paper to Monica. The car that Anthony was driving belonged to her. He'd had his own car until recently but it was old and not worth repairing. We sold it with the understanding that he could only use his mother's car for work and when he absolutely needed a vehicle.

Monica looked at the photos and cried. She too was concerned with if and how much our poor boy suffered.

Then the phone rang. Who it was I don't recall because from that point on, the phone rang constantly. As one of us spoke on the phone we could hear the beep tone indicating another call was incoming. Then another and another. The special tone that indicates a voice mail would sound over and over again.

The doorbell rang. It was our friend Glenn. He has a daughter who attended school with Anthony from grade school through to college. He offered his condolences with the words we would hear over and over for a long time; "I just can't imagine" and "I don't know what to say".
From that moment there would be a constant stream of friends and family coming in and out of the house as well as phone calls, text messages, emails, flower and food deliveries.

I remember thinking, that first day after the accident, I thought," we have to notify people that may not know. Monica was first to start the calls. I overheard her speaking to someone. "Hello Sandra, you'd better sit down, I have some bad news. Anthony has passed". There was a pause and then she repeated, "Anthony has passed". It didn't sound like Sandra understood. "Passed what", I believe she said. We had to be more direct in telling people.

I got on the phone to tell my friend Andy. His wife Sheryl answered.

"Sheryl", I said.

"Anthony was killed in a car accident last night".

"What"? She responded in disbelief.

"Anthony was killed by a suspected drunk driver in a police chase last night".

"What"? She repeated with pain in her voice and not wanting to hear the words.

Andy had the phone now.

"What happened"?

Anthony was killed in a car accident last night", I said, feeling my eyes well up.

I don't remember the rest of that conversation, or many of the ones that were to follow. I had to be blunt. I couldn't soften the words and risk confusion. My son was dead and a lot of people needed to know.

People have a wonderful comforting habit of gathering when a death has occurred to support the bereaved in any way they can. Everyone does this. I believe it serves a number of purposes. People want to support the grieving family, simply by "being there" with them. People like to share grief. They have a sense of helping by sharing the grief of friends. It also serves to console people who haven't lost a family member but who know the deceased.

And then there's the food, everybody wanted to bring us food.

"They won't be in any state to cook so let's bring them something". It seems that ninety percent of the time, they bring Lasagna. Lasagna in all flavors and sizes and most often oversized.

Now, don't get me wrong. I have never in my life experienced a greater outpouring of support and affection. It came from people I know well and from people I don't know that well at all. But the food, my God, the colossal amounts of food! Lasagna, cookies, cakes, casseroles, soft drinks, buns, coffee and more coffee. Some of its still in our freezer, even one year after the accident. Some people got creative.

"I thought we'd bring food", said one good friend. "And we brought some of the things that go with it, like napkins, disposable cups and cutlery".

I was grateful that I had bought a full sized, stand up freezer a few years before. Otherwise I'd have had to throw out a good deal of that great food. And, in addition to the food, we suddenly had three times as much Tupperware too.

We'd received so much Lasagna that Alanna blurted out at dinner a few days later, "Is Lasagna death food? Is there some social rule dictating that people are supposed to bring Lasagna to families that lose loved ones"?
Finally something that made us laugh, which generated pangs of guilt in me. My son is dead and I am laughing. He would have laughed at that too, I thought.

Anthony's teachers came over with food. They too shed tears. His boss from the restaurant where Anthony had worked brought food. Lots of it. Greek salad and yes, more lasagna. He could hardly contain his tears as he told me, "You know, we have a lot of kids working at the restaurant and I hear all of the dumb things they say and talk about, but I never heard Anthony say any of the typical dumb things that kids talk about, he was a really good kid".

I thought to myself during those first few days that perhaps grief would curb my appetite and I'd lose a bit of weight. I lost a few pounds at first but they didn't stay off for long. Again, it's funny the things you think about at a time like that.

All of the food that people brought us was greatly appreciated and all devoured.
Then there were the flowers. We had so many bouquets of flowers; it was difficult to find room for them all but we appreciated all of them.
All I can say now is that I have a great dislike of the smell of fresh flowers.

The influx of well-wishers went on for 3 days but it seemed like much longer. I remember it got to the point where good friends would come in the house, their eyes full of tears and I'd end up consoling them. "It's OK, it's OK", I said to my friend Jim.
"No its not", he replied, pulling back from me and looking at me with his red, watery eyes. I have to admit it became difficult after a while. People were continually streaming through the door. They had large bouquets of flowers and food. All of them were saying exactly the same thing. "Here, I thought you might need some food so I brought you some Lasagna".

"Oh, thank you, that's very kind of you", I'd say with a smile. Later, I would share our newfound Lasagna humor with these people. It's a good thing too. Some of them may be reading this book. I don't want to offend their incredible kindness.

It finally became apparent to the three of us how tired we were getting. People were constantly coming and going, making coffee, cleaning up and putting things away. They had good intentions but it was very busy. We needed some time alone to figure out what to do next and get some rest.

I distinctly remember someone saying to Monica and me, "you know, it's OK to put a sign on the door that says, "We are mourning in private today as a family, thank you for your understanding".

"If you don't, you'll go out of your minds", the person said.

Could we really do that, I thought?

I crafted a small sign and taped it to the door and closed the curtains. We felt horrible when we could hear people at the door and then leave after reading the sign. But it had to be done for our own sanity. Anyone reading this who has experienced a similar situation will understand.

In the days following the accident, the media called and called and called. My instinct told me to be extremely careful with the media. They can turn a good story into a bad one with a single sentence. No one was going to make my son look bad. Initially, Monica said that she didn't want to do any interviews. Alanna disagreed and emphatically said, "No, I want the world to know how good a brother he was. I want to be interviewed".

And that was when the media circus started. I must say that my fears never came to pass. Every one of them were kind and compassionate and wrote wonderful and touching stories about our Anthony.

It seemed that when one media agency called, like a newspaper or radio station, two or three additional media organizations would call within an hour or two. I realized months later that the media feed from the same trough. Which particular trough, I don't know. This has continued right up to the time of writing this book some 9 months since the accident.

So, you can imagine, people coming and going in droves, bringing more food. Then the media would call.

"We're in the neighborhood, can we come over for a quick interview"?

I assumed that if they said they were in the neighborhood and we declined then we'd feel guilty. We welcomed them no matter whose neighborhood they were in.

All of this continued for days and we had little knowledge of what was going on outside of the confines of our home. We didn't know it at the time but there was activity related to Anthony's death going on throughout the community. A roadside memorial had been erected by his friends at the crash scene within hours. Extremely touching memorial videos were created and posted on social media sites. The first of which, Monica would play numerous times to guests and members of the media. It was a pictorial of beautiful photos of Anthony at school and with friends. The music in the background was about being strong and was a perfect piece for the video. It was created by a young man named Justin. I had never heard of him and only met him during the onslaught when he came for a quick visit. It also brought everyone who watched it to tears.

There were bumper stickers being printed and sold. Bracelets were made and sold to friends. The students at his former high school and the college he was attending at the time were organizing events in support of our son.

We live in a small house. On the ground floor, one side is the kitchen and eat-in area. The other side is living/dining room. We had to put friends who dropped in on the kitchen side. The living/dining room became the "studio". Because we live in Quebec, interviews were conducted in English and then French. The English TV interview, then the French TV interview, the English radio interview, then the French radio interview. We would often do four interviews a day, with friends and family watching from the entrance to the kitchen. We also shed a lot of tears during those interviews.

Monica mentioned one very important thing during our first interview. Something that I am so proud of, the interviewer asked, "So tell me, as a parent, how are you feeling about the loss of your son"?
Monica's reply was typical of her kind and generous heart. "Well, you must understand. Two families lost sons that night. We did and the Campbell family did. So I want to extend our condolences to the family and friends of Brian Campbell".

This seemed to send a shock wave through the community. Suddenly we were an "inspiration" to everyone for being so strong and forgiving.

At the end of the first day of interviews, Monica and I reflected on that thought.

The question came up. Were we angry with Brian Campbell, the 21 year old who killed our son? I thought about that for a very long time. To this day I harbor no anger, hate or feelings of vengeance toward this young man. Why, I don't know. If asked prior to my son's death what I'd do in similar circumstances, my answer would probably not have been so gracious and forgiving. I guess you don't know until you are faced with this type of thing how you'll react. I'm happy with the way we did react.

Campbell didn't intend to kill my son that night. He simply made some bad choices. Both he and my son paid the ultimate price for those choices. If anyone says, "how can you be so strong", I simply tell them, that even though it's expected and acceptable for people to feel some anger, we just don't. Adding anger and hate to the tremendous weight of grief of losing a child would make life unbearable. Quite simply it will shorten our lives. We must get on with living. We have a desire and an obligation to have our story be known, to try to prevent others from living the same pain we live every day. I don't know how we came to feel this way. We didn't have a pre-arranged plan on how we would

—

present our feelings toward the Campbell family in public. During the numerous interviews we simply offered our sincere condolences to the Campbell family, because they lost their son as well. If, through our awareness efforts, we can save one life, then we will have been successful. I know already that lives have been saved.

We continued to conduct interviews for the print media and various television and radio shows with a positive attitude. A natural consequence of our son being killed in an automobile accident is that we now notice every news article related to car crashes. What were the circumstances? Were there any deaths? I almost always send condolences to the family and friends of the deceased as I've been keeping up on these continuing and too numerous accidents; I've noticed a number of things. The most prevalent is that our situation could have been much worse. Anthony's passengers were hurt: two, very seriously. All have healed at least physically to this point. The car could have caught on fire. They may not have wearing their seat belts. Brian Campbell wasn't wearing his seat belt. However Anthony always said, "buckle up everyone", before driving anywhere. I've always been a stickler for safety. I constantly drill it into my children's heads to buckle up. Sadly, seat belts can't save a person in all circumstances. We learned this through Anthony's death.

I found out that, milliseconds prior to impact, my son turned the car slightly away from Campbell's on-coming car. It meant he would take the majority of the impact. In the months following the accident, I had the opportunity to inspect both cars in great detail. I even took photographs. The impact of the crash must have been tremendous. Many people have seen my photographs of the car. They've asked how I could bring myself to do that. I simply told them that I had to get a close look at the place where my son took his final breath. We learned that he died on impact, which was confirmed by the first responders who were at the crash scene that night.

I touched the driver's seat, the steering wheel and the entire car hoping that perhaps I might feel a shimmer of his spirit. All I felt was cold metal, broken glass and unrecognizable scraps of plastic.

I made a second trip to examine the wreckage to retrieve personal items that the girls were asking about. I found three cell phones, two pairs of sunglasses, purses and my son's favorite backpack. It was an orange and black tartan patterned snowboard pack. My wife now uses it sometimes when she goes to the gym to work out. It makes her feel like he is with her.

One of the cell phones was Anthony's. It was an iPhone that he'd treasured. Surprisingly it still worked. The car had been left out in the elements for weeks. The phone was wet when I found it. I brought it home and turned it on. Immediately it started to vibrate and flash with messages. I opened the messages and started to read starting on April 15.

There were the usual messages, asking what's up, are you going here or there, type of messages. I scrolled closer to the time of the accident, which was 2:30 AM, Saturday, April 16. One message made me tremble with shock. The message was from a friend around 5:00 AM, April 16.

It read, "Hey Tony, I hear Chelsea was in a bad car accident last night. Do you know anything about that"?

Anthony had been dead for two and a half hours by then. Another string of messages I read was later that morning from the same sender. The string started by asking how's it going.

The final message was, "Hey Tony, how come you're not answering my messages, I'm starting to get worried. Call me man".

Then the content of the messages turned to messages of love and condolences.

I turned the phone off. I couldn't listen anymore, nor could I read the messages through my tears. My Anthony was never coming home.

In time, the visits slowed to a trickle. We continued to eat the food brought to us by wonderful friends and family. Our minds finally turned to what we had to do next; what happens with the insurance? What do we put in the obituary? What about the funeral arrangements?

What we wanted to know most of all were the details leading up to the crash?

I started to think about something that Monica had taught me many years earlier. It was about getting closure. It was something that would help me in the days and months ahead. I had found a new job. It meant leaving my current employer whom I'd been with a number of years. I'd had difficulty "letting go". Moving on to my new employer proved a slow transition. Being a career Social Worker, Monica had been good at seeing things that maybe slowed my forward momentum. I thought about this a lot in our endeavors to get all of the things done related to our son's death. It helped me with the constant waves of shock and grief that all three of us were continually bombarded with.

A death related to a car accident comes with added baggage. There are many things to consider when dealing with death related to a car accident. Not only do you have to deal with family and friends but with the insurance company, the police report, the media and the families of the occupants of the car. Not to mention the family of Brian Campbell, the other victim of this tragic accident. We wondered what his family was going through.

I contacted the insurance company. I'm sure all auto insurance companies have a division that deals with death and serious injury. These people were extremely compassionate in all of my conversations with them. Being a stickler for customer service and experiencing very poor customer service on too many occasions, I was surprised by the excellent treatment I received.

We were offered a free car rental to use in place of our vehicle, which was a relief. The provincial insurance people were helpful as well. There were reams of documents to complete. Proof of education, proof of employment, social insurance number, the death certificate, the cremation certificate, collecting personal possessions from the police, etc. There are a lot of documents. Each one is a point of closure. Get it done and move on to the next task. Being a goal oriented person; I felt that these closure points helped me in dealing with my grief. Don't get me wrong. Getting through these closure points didn't mean I was getting over my son's death. It merely meant that I cleared a painful hurdle that is another one of the many sad tasks necessary when dealing with a death. I'll never "get over" my son's death. I'm just better able to deal with his death by completing these tasks and getting them out of the way.

I began to call all of these items "death errands". They are tasks associated with "closing the books" on a person's life. A partial list is available in Addendum A

In my mind, each of these "closure points" represented a small step toward being better able to cope with the death of a child. They're pretty much one time things to do and you shouldn't have to re-visit them again. Then there are the "firsts". The first Christmas where your loved one is absent, the first birthday without him or her, the first anniversary of the accident. The first birthday of your loved one after they have passed. These will obviously be repeated as the years go by, but the first time they come around can be very difficult.

We are a very close family. Being together is everything. "I don't care what I do for a living or how much money I make. My wealth has always been defined by my family", I always used to say. "No matter what, as long as the 4 of us are together, I'm a millionaire". Where I go from this point is difficult to handle. I must mourn my son's death while at the same time make sure my wife and daughter aren't short changed by my grief.

The Visitation and Funeral

We decided to have the visitation at a larger funeral home for a number of reasons. Beside the fact that our local funeral home is very small, there was road construction going on in the neighborhood. It would have been next to impossible for guests to find parking. Not to mention the fact that the price difference between the two was literally thousands of dollars.

Another thing we also had to consider was whether it would be an open or closed coffin. We knew we had to resist the overpowering pull of grief to focus on this important task. Monica was adamant, "I insist on having an open coffin. There are going to be a lot of young people coming, I want them to see that when someone makes a bad decision, young people die"!

I agreed. Since Anthony didn't have any visible facial injuries, it would be fairly simple to opt for an open coffin. We knew this would be disturbing for a lot of people. It was.

Now that I've gone through this experience I'd suggest that you might want to consult a friend that has gone through funeral arranging in the past. There are so many things to consider and a hurried decision could cost you a lot of money unnecessarily. Even getting a keepsake that contains a small portion of your loved ones ashes could cost you hundreds of dollars.

The visitation, it turns out was scheduled for Easter Sunday, April 24, 2011. Yes, Easter. How convenient for everyone (not). I remember thinking, "who is going to be there, they'll all be out at Easter brunch enjoying a lovely spring day". Celebrate Easter by going to a wake for a 19 year old, killed in a violent car crash.
I couldn't have been more wrong.
April 24 turned out to be a sunny, warm spring day. It seemed like the first really nice day since winter. Over 1,000 people showed up. There was a line that snaked out the door of the funeral home and around the building. People waited two hours in line to come in, offer their condolences and then enter the room to see my beautiful boy in a grey steel coffin.

When my sister went outside to see how many people were in line, I told her to let people know that they can just come in another door and go and see Anthony. They didn't have to wait in line. No one did. They all decided to stay in line and greet Monica, Alanna and me. How utterly humbling.

The visitation was from 2:00 PM to 7:00 PM. I later found out that people would come by in their cars, see the line up and then decide to come back later when the line up had subsided. When they returned they were surprised to see the line up was still as long as it had been hours earlier. It was truly amazing.

We encouraged everyone to enter the room and say a final goodbye. Most did, some couldn't bring themselves to enter the room. Some of Anthony's closest friends remained the entire afternoon, often getting very close to the coffin. Some even reached in and gave Anthony one last hug goodbye. It was difficult for a lot of people. But it made me understand how important it was to have the coffin open.

Monica, Alanna and I stood there and greeted these kind, generous and patient people from 1:45 to 7:15 PM. In the end we had to subtly give the remaining people the boot. We were exhausted. The funeral was to be held the next day. People left cards some with cheques in them. In the coming months we would use this money for the "Tony's Promise" campaign.

The Funeral

The funeral was held on Monday, April 25, Easter Monday. Our very dear friend Peggy handled all of the details surrounding the funeral. She is a long time parishioner and knows the priest well. Peggy stick-handled everything from arranging the music to the food and refreshments being served afterwards in the church basement. I thought that since so many people paid their respects during the visitation, we'd be lucky to get 100 people at the funeral. Once again I was wrong. Close to 600 people showed up at the church. The church holds approximately 300. We managed to stuff in about 400. Close to 200 people stood outside for the entire funeral. The police were called in to close the main street to ensure the safety of the grieving crowd. The press showed up as well - two television crews and two newspaper crews. It was certainly news worthy. Against the advice of her doctor, Lea, the most seriously injured in the crash attended the funeral in a wheelchair. There was a lineup outside the church, just like the visitation. I knew that not everyone would get a seat. So, I made my way around the outside of the church, shaking hands and thanking everyone for coming. I finally reached the end of the line minutes before the service was to start. I went to shake hands with the very last person in the line.

It was Dr. Barrett Adams, Anthony's Pediatrician.

I thanked him for coming and for all of the care he had given to my son over his first 18 years. I also mentioned that he probably wouldn't get into the church. He looked understandably sad and apologized for being late.

I almost burst into tears at the sight of Dr. Adams but my responsibility was to the 600 people who'd come to say their final goodbye to Anthony. I was determined to make sure this funeral went well and that everyone knew how honored and thankful we were.

The ceremony was very touching. The mother of one of Anthony's friends plays the bagpipes and she offered to "pipe" him into and out of the church. We had 11 of his best friends as pallbearers. In the days leading up to the funeral I was adamant that I would write and present the eulogy. I had a lot to say about my son and the great support we were getting from our friends and the community. When I sat down to write it, I drew a complete blank and wrote only two sentences. I was at a loss. I started to think about all of the interviews I had done with Monica and Alanna and was running out of steam. Monica said that she would like to write the eulogy, and she did. It was beautiful and I'm so glad she wrote it. I stood at the podium with her while she delivered it.

Eulogy

What a beautiful and brilliant outpouring of support and love this community, our families and friends have shown for us and for our son, Anthony, "Tony".

All week we have felt wrapped in that love, and we thank you so much. It has helped us get through this horrendous week.

Anthony was a spirited child who was extra sensitive and felt things intensely, both physically and emotionally; to the point of our having to cut the labels out of his t-shirts. We had to because he would literally pull them off himself and ruin the shirt.

As a toddler, he had the strength of a child much older and the will and determination of 10 adults. It was very difficult to dissuade him from his path... But we soon discovered that tickling; galloping around the room (he called it galpowing!) or playing with water would do the trick. He was extremely gregarious. It was always hard to get him to come for dinner from playing outside. He would say: "But Mummy, we are planing!" like it was an imperative or a calling or something...

He loved his friends and their adventures. He was a loyal and kind friend.

He was very sensitive to others. In grade 6, they watched the movie "Life is Beautiful" for a project on the Second World War and he cried. It touched him. Only after, did he think he should not have, because he got razzed for it. But he soon got back to the place of feeling it had been OK to cry at such a sad movie...

I loved his hands. Big, beautiful, elegant and so strong; yet he could perform extremely intricate, precise and delicate work with them. Always conscious of his strength, so he took pains to be extra tender and careful with them.

I was never so proud of Anthony than when he was introduced to an elder or someone less appreciated in society. He would bend down because he was almost always far taller than them; take their hand in his (knowing that his touch could relay comfort) and looked into their eyes with respect and humility. His smile told them so much.

He had a lot of time with my mother who adored him. She was his caregiver from the age of 6 months to 2 and a half years, when I went back to work. Every evening, when I went to pick him up, the state of her house would tell me that he had had a lovely day: all the pots were out of the cupboards, he was drumming, or the house was strewn with clothes and blankets, he was playing dress-up or building forts. She never fussed about the mess. They were so good for each other. The love he received was multigenerational. He cherished those days with her as she did with him.

Then I was able to stay home for 6 years with him and his sister, Alanna. We had lots of fun at LaLeche league, Aylmer community playgroups and at the local public park and pool (which is what they call Manoirs des Trembles these days) and at so many friends' homes and backyards. We went to that park 3 times a day, mornings, after naptime and in the evening.... We had such lovely times inventing the Anthony song, the Alanna song, going to Artissimo at the National Gallery. At 4 years of age, he went through a large craft store called "White Rose", brandishing a sign he had made, chanting, "Vote for Anthony! Vote for Anthony!" (We are not sure what he was running for...)

He was a whiz at puzzles. My sister related an incident when she had got him a big puzzle that she felt he could grow into and showed him how to place the first few pieces. She said he just looked at her with some puzzlement and simply proceeded to place every piece in order one after the other within moments. His look then was of: "You are going to have to get me something more difficult than this..." As a teacher, she said, "let me see, I wrote this down.... his visual spatial awareness was uncanny".

*His kindness and soft heartedness was legendary at our house.
If someone came to the door; maybe a little disheveled and
looking for a job, raking leaves or something, at 8 years' old,
Anthony plead with me: "please Mummy, say yes, don't turn
him away."*

*In his teens, he made it clear that he did not like phonies or
posers, as he called them. That is, people who put more effort
into things and social standing than effort into people.*

*He went a little anti-establishment wearing Che Guevara t-
shirts and listening to "Rage Against the Machine" music. For
which I was secretly so proud. I knew that if I showed my
approval, the opposite teen-parent dynamic would be upset.
It's only anti-establishment, if your old fogey parents think its
wrong....*

*He had so much potential at school, at rugby, in the arts,
acting, singing, making music, videos and films... But lots of
times, he did not seem to know it himself.*

*When a son gets to a certain age, he starts to live a more
independent adult life where he doesn't share all with his
parents. Which Anthony did in the last 2 years or so. It has been
very gratifying to meet the people from that part of Anthony's*

life. It confirmed that he made good decisions.

What pains me the most is that all his potential will not come to fruition through an entire life to middle age and old age.

I am here to give tribute to my son. Others have done so as well. There was a wonderful tribute to Anthony on Tuesday night at Heritage College where it seemed more than 20 acts of song, poetry, and readings honored "Tony" for 4 hours and was attended by 400 participants. Thank you again to those who put that together! It has helped our family go on...

Others have erected a memorial at the crash site with crosses made for Tony. It has been very gratifying to discover in such a concrete way, just how much Anthony was loved and appreciated by his friends. Not to mention, the Tony's Promise campaign on Face book that is already doing so much good.

All from love and kindness, which is what, I believe, Anthony was about; it was his most striking legacy.

It is what we, David, Alanna and I have made the decision to be about. We need to support one another and put differences and jealousies aside. Love each other in deed and in word.

Now <u>we</u> have to be the guardians of what Anthony brought to the world.

Your father, your sister and I will miss you, my darling Anthony!

Love always,
Your Mum

Homily delivered by Father Bill Marevee of St. Mark the Evangelist Church, Aylmer, Quebec

Difficult circumstances bring us here together. I can only surmise what goes on in your hearts, Monica and Dave and Alanna now that Anthony is so abruptly taken away from you. Yes, you have lots of fond memories of his 19 years in your midst, memories that you will now cherish even more. It must be painful to realize that there will be no additional memories. Please, know, Monica and David, that we all are impressed and thankful for the nobility and grace with which you have spoken, in private and in public, of Brian Campbell and of his family.

Still, Anthony's sudden and tragic death at such an early age leaves us all shaken, bewildered, cheated. We do not understand. If anything, it shows how at times life can be unreasonable, unfair. This does not fit in anyone's design.... It does not fit in God's design either. If Anthony's sudden death is heart breaking for his parents, sister and loved ones, it is heart breaking for God as well. God does not want this either. Considering the place we are in, it is quite appropriate that we let God know about our confusion and bewilderment. I am confident that we find a listening ear, above all, a listening heart.

Allow me to say a few words to Anthony's peers, his many friends. You are here in great numbers. I have the sense that you cherished Anthony's presence in your lives, and that Anthony cherished your presence in his life. That makes his death all the more bewildering for you, a devastating experience for you. After all, he is one of your own. It must raise all sorts of strange and difficult questions as it does for all of us.

Life is a precious gift. You are at a stage where you begin to taste its enjoyments, its challenges, its possibilities. Supported by those who love you and care for you are at the point of taking ownership of it, of planning for your future. And now you come face to face with the fact that the precious gift of life is also a very fragile and vulnerable gift, even to the point that it can be taken from us without any apparent rhyme or reason. Take good care of the precious gift of your life; take good care of each other and of all those you meet on life's journey. You do so by the various initiatives you have undertaken this past week, which are so thoughtful, generous and caring. They tell us that life for every one of us is just too precious and too fragile to be taken for granted.

Over the past week we have come together in different places to seek comfort in each other's presence. We needed to do this.

Now we have come together in this place where we seek God's presence in these difficult circumstances. I am not suggesting that God is limited to this place, but here we put our search for God – a God who at times can appear to be so distant --, here we put our search for God in focus. We bring before God our bewilderment, our confusion. Above all, we bring before God Anthony now that he has died; we bring before God Monica and David and Alanna in their pain and sadness.

And look where we have placed Anthony: Right under the Cross and the Easter Candle. They speak to us of the Crucified and Risen Jesus. Jesus is God's gift of compassion, of suffering-with-us, God not so distant but close to us. This past week we have celebrated that Jesus gave his life for us, for Anthony; he was raised from the dead for us, for Anthony to let us know that death, however real, is not the last word about us, about Anthony. All of us, today especially Anthony, we are too precious in God's eyes to let the grip that death now has on Anthony be a lasting one. In Jesus, dead and risen, God wrestles Anthony free from the grip that death has on him. I know this goes beyond our understanding and it does not take away the pain and darkness Anthony's death causes. Still, it reminds us that there is one reality that is greater than the darkness of death: it is the God of Jesus who loves Anthony, who loves us. To that God we cling, albeit with tears and a heavy heart.

Together we give Anthony over to God; we speak our à-Dieu over him and we pray that in the embrace of the life-giving God Anthony may find the peace and life to which the gracious God summons us all. And we pray for Monica and David and Alanna, and for ourselves that Anthony's death may not make us cynical or bitter about life. We pray that, instead, God's love and compassion may help us see through the darkness that now envelopes our hearts. We want to support each other as we place our confidence and our hope in the life-giving and people-loving God.

Anthony, rest in peace. À-Dieu.

There wasn't a dry eye in the entire church.

Close to the end of the ceremony there was a gasp from the back of the church. People started calling for a doctor. I got up to see what was going on. Someone had collapsed. I got closer and saw it was the 18-year-old son of a close family friend. He had fainted. Seeing that he was in good hands with a doctor and two nurses I headed back to my seat. I said to Monica, "It's Colin, he's tough, he'll be OK". Colin is a strong and skilled hockey player, he was up and fine a few minutes later.

The service finished. The pallbearers gathered around the coffin in tears. A look of utter devastation was on all of their faces. Anthony's baptismal scarf was draped across the coffin.

I was proud of those guys.

Monica, Alanna and I followed the piper out of the church to a throng of family, friends and media.

The coffin was placed in the hearse, protruding out the back a bit. We wanted to be able to touch Anthony's coffin so we could publicly say our last goodbyes. We put our hands on the coffin. Monica and Alanna were in tears. I wanted to have a moment but I was far too distracted by the cameras, the people, the police and the shock. I leaned over and draped my arms around the coffin. I wanted it to feel like I was hugging my son for the last time. All I felt was how uncomfortable it was putting my arms around this large, grey, steel box.

All of a sudden I remember thinking "this isn't the coffin we ordered. We distinctly ordered a coffin made of oak". I decided not to worry about it until later. Days after the funeral, I enquired at the funeral home as to the change in coffin. They told me was that because of Anthony's size, he didn't fit into the oak coffin. So they went ahead with the larger grey metal one instead. A good choice we thought, heavy metal. It also matched the color of the hearse perfectly.

After the funeral ceremony, there was the usual refreshment function in the church basement. It seemed that everyone came downstairs for a sandwich and a coffee. I couldn't believe the amount of food! There was far more than necessary and I was thankful for that. Although I managed to eat very little, I was too busy talking to everyone.

When someone dies usually people at the funeral want desperately to say something comforting. It's normal and natural for people to want to do something or say something that will ease your pain. Some say nothing for fear of increasing your pain. Although what that could be I can only imagine. Some speak when they shouldn't. One gentleman, the boyfriend/partner of a woman I know and claiming to be a doctor, approached and started talking to me. He proceeded to tell me how he couldn't find a job. Hmmm, I thought, I've never heard of a doctor that couldn't find a job, how odd. He then continued. I'm sure he meant to make me feel better by telling me about an acquaintance of his who had lost a child in some tragic way. He then went on to inform me that a year later the same family lost the second child to some accident or disease.

A word of advice, don't say that to someone at the funeral of his or her child.

I needed a sandwich, and fast.

A few moments later Anthony's rugby team complete with team jerseys got up on the stage and sang "Amazing Grace". One verse in the traditional manner and one in the "hardcore/metal" style in honor of the style of music he played in his band "Hostility".

It was starting to become another long day.

After a few hours, people finally cleared out of the church basement. We headed home to relax. Or, that is what I recall. My memory told me that after the funeral I went straight home with my family. I found out over one year later that this was not the case. Almost a year and a half after Anthony's death, Monica and I were at the home of our dear friends, Peggy and Rick Henderson for dinner. We got to discussing the crash, as we often do with the Henderson's, and the topic of the funeral came up. We chatted about the number of people there, the media, etc. And I mentioned that it was good to get home after the funeral because I was exhausted and hungry. Peggy suddenly looked up at me and said, "You didn't go home after the funeral. You came here. Don't you remember that"?

I thought about that Easter Monday so long ago. I dug deep into my memory of the day and looking at Peggy said, "No, I don't remember that".

"You, Monica, the Wilsons and your sister and brother-in-law came here for a drink and a quick bite to eat."

I stared at Peggy in disbelief.

She said that the reason she remembers that so well is that Monica looked at a photo of Peggy's one-year-old grandson Miller, and broke down in tears. She spoke of never being able to be the grandmother of Anthony's children now. "You don't remember that"?

"I think I remember being here", I said with hesitation, not recalling any of it.

I couldn't remember that and still don't as of the writing of these words.

"Well, being in your house Peggy is like being at home for me anyway. You have been so incredibly supportive of us."

Grief induced shock is a powerful and scary thing.

Who Was My Son

Anthony was a planned child. Monica and I wanted to have children of course but wanted to be ready and prepared when the time came. I had been working in the corporate travel industry for many years and we could travel anywhere in the world at relatively low cost. We travelled around North America and Europe until we had our fill and started planning. So in 1991, we planned our last vacation before embarking on the "baby" train.

Monica wanted a vacation on a beach somewhere exotic so she could relax completely and not have to do anything except eat, sleep and get a tan, as if she knew the amount of work it would take to raise a son. I connected with my industry colleagues, worked out a great airfare and we spent 2 beautiful weeks in Greece. While there we met and befriended a lot of people. One such group was from South Africa. Two young men named Micky and Antony as well as Micky's sister and a friend of hers. It turned out they were on a working vacation, getting a job at the beach camping area where we stayed on our first week on the island of Mykonos. We got to know them quite well. Monica was particularly impressed by Antony, or "Ant" as his friends called him. He was good looking and a perfect gentleman. I remember after a good conversation we had with these fine young people Monica said to me, "I·think if we have a son, we should call him Antony after that fine young South African man". I agreed. I can still recall his chiseled facial features and polite demeanor.

Our Anthony (we inadvertently left the "h" in there when naming him) was born on Wednesday, March 11, 1992 at 11:30 PM. It snowed incessantly all day. I was originally scheduled to be on a corporate ski trip that day, a few hours out of town, but that was cancelled due to the treacherous driving conditions. I happily wouldn't have made it either way.

Monica had been scheduled to have labor induced due to complications with Anthony's size, in utero. He was always big. He was a big fetus, a big baby and a big man.

The nurse injected Monica with labor inducing petocin at 8:30 AM. Her labor was slow and painful. As the ignorant, first time father, there wasn't much I could do. And, of course, whatever I offered was politely handled by the nurses and refused by Monica. At one point the nurse said, "You should go and get a coffee". Why she said that I have no idea, I wasn't doing anything or getting in the way. I went to the cafeteria and got myself a hazelnut-flavored coffee. I got back to the room and a few minutes later Monica said, "you know the smell of that coffee is really bothering me".

Off I went again to step outside of the main entrance of the hospital and let the howling wind and snow smack me around. It was evening and dark out. I wore no coat or hat, just a tee shirt, jeans and running shoes. It was quite refreshing and I remember wondering if I should feel any stress or not. I was certainly tired but snapped back to reality as I thought of the obvious pain Monica was going through. Birth is a messy business, blood, pain and in our case, a whole lot of waiting.

Earlier on that day a young couple were assigned to the bed next to Monica's in the staging area for mothers about to give birth. Two hours later our nurse informed us that the couple had a lovely baby boy and were off to their room.

"That's not fair", said Monica.

"We were here before they were", as if to imply that babies should be born in the order that the parents arrive at the hospital. I didn't respond to that out of concern for my own physical safety.

At approximately 10:00 PM the doctor broached the topic of Caesarian Section. Monica had been loosing blood and had been in and out of contractions for over 10 hours at this point. She had also been in a lot of pain.

"Well, you're not dilating enough for a natural birth so we should consider a C section", said the doctor.

"Unfortunately we don't have anyone who can give you an epidural so you'll have to go under a general anesthetic".

"Well, I don't like the sound of that". Replied Monica.

"I want to see my baby being born".

"Well it doesn't look good for an epidural, I'm sorry".

So, Monica was wheeled into the operating room and I followed.

"You go in there and put on these", said the nurse as she handed me the usual hospital blue pants shirt and booties.

"Stay in here and we'll come get you when we're ready".

I was in a locker room. I guessed this is where the doctors, staff and useless fathers go to get ready prior to baby delivery.

After what seemed to be too long a time, the nurse came in and said,

"We're ready for you".

I followed and entered a typical looking operating room full of people and machines making beeps and humming.

To my surprise Monica was not under anesthesia. She was lying on a gurney with a man sitting next to her.

"This man is God", she said.

"We found the person that gives epidurals", said Monica's doctor.

"I'm telling you this man is God, I have absolutely no pain, I love this man".

Looking up at the doctor who gave her the epidural, Monica added, "You don't know me, I don't like doctors, but I really like you".

"Ok, so your happy... that's good", I said cautiously.

I was very happy to see that she was no longer in pain and that we would finally see our Anthony.

I was instructed to remain sitting next to Monica's head and comfort her. No small task with "God" sitting on the other side of her.

Anyway, they proceeded to conduct the C-section and in a minute or two a big, chubby, beautiful, blue baby boy was brought to our end of the bed.

My Anthony was born and he was beautiful. Of course, due to the drop in temperature between the womb and the delivery room, Ant was shocked by this sudden change and proceeded to urinate, sending a small arching stream throughout the delivery/operating room.

That's my boy. Make a statement early in life, I thought.

He was close to nine pounds at birth and since Monica suffered gestational diabetes during her pregnancy, the hospital took precautions and monitored Ant for diabetes as soon as he was born. This meant that they had to keep him in an incubator for a few days, just until they determined he wasn't at risk of diabetes. Now, usually incubators are reserved for premature births, which, as we all know are babies that are almost always very tiny.

The day after Ant was born, we had a few visits from family and friends. They would come to our room and, as Monica was in bed recuperating from C-section surgery, I would proudly escort visitors down the hall to look in the window of the maternity ward to see Ant. It was quite a site for visitors to see all of the tiny three pound "preemies" in the incubators and then I'd hear a gasp as their eyes landed on Anthony. He was quite out of place. He looked as if he were a moving sardine packed in a tin trying to squeeze out of the confines of this little incubator, surrounded by all of these newborns that were the size of his leg. His size would be a bone of contention for him for a lot of his short life.

His strength was nothing short of amazing right from the moment he was born.

The hospital room was full of the usual neonatal paraphernalia including a little change table. This change table had a metal railing along the edge. Clearly designed to prevent our little one from rolling off of the table during diaper changes. Knowing how weak and fragile newborns are, it was difficult to imagine a five hour old baby being able to roll over. Since Monica was pretty much unable to get out of bed for the first day or two, I was in charge of the first diaper changes. I laid Anthony on the change table and proceeded to change him. I took off the old, soggy diaper and tossed it in the receptacle. As I reached for a new diaper he grabbed the metal railing and was so strong that he essentially did a "curl", you know the thing a weightlifter does with a dumbbell and was about to pull himself off of the change table. Fortunately I put my hand on him and stopped that excursion.

Later in the day after a feeding, I started to rock him. He was upright with his head on my shoulder. He fidgeted a little and I stopped rocking. With my hand on his back, he lifted his head up and away from my shoulder. Now that is a strong baby.

We brought him home after a few days and thought, OK, now what do we do? We have our first child, are we ready to look after a helpless, tiny thing that completely and utterly depends on Monica and me to look after him? The thought was frightening.

But we're human and humans have been doing this for millions of years.

Monica was determined that he would be a breast-fed baby and in the hospital she had a lot of difficulty getting him to "latch" on to her breast. "Latch" is the term used when the baby has the nipple properly inserted into his or her mouth and can draw milk properly. If you don't get a proper latch, the baby doesn't get milk and it can be painful for the mother. Eventually, Monica contacted a group called the La Leche League. Their mission is;

"To encourage, promote and provide mother-to-mother breastfeeding support and educational opportunities as an important contribution to the health of children, families and society". **http://www.lllc.ca/**

She contacted the local group and was invited to attend a session at the nearby home of a La Leche specialist. We put Anthony in his car seat, hopped into the car and drove the five minutes to a house a few blocks away. Upon arrival, we got out of the car, went to the door, Monica with the baby in the car seat ahead of me. A woman answered the door, invited Monica in and abruptly put her hand up and in my face saying, "no men allowed", and shut the door.

From that point on, I affectionately referred to them as "the breast feeding nuts".

It wasn't long before Anthony got the latch and fed pretty much every two hours round the clock for nine months. I'm also happy to say that some of the babies in those La Leche League sessions became good friends with Anthony, friendships that lasted right up to the time of his death.

As the months went by, Anthony grew, and grew and grew some more. He took his first steps at nine months old. I have his first steps on video somewhere in the boxes of stored books and DVDs.

It wasn't long before we discovered what a "spirited child" was, and he was the epitome of a spirited child. He wanted to do everything and he wanted to do it right now! This desire to do everything would carry on for many years. He could climb anything as well. One day Monica walked into the kitchen to find a three-year-old Anthony waving an 8-inch Henckel knife. As she walked toward him in shock, she said, "what are you doing sweetie"?

"I'm a piwate (pirate)", he responded saying it in a tone that a pirate would use. The only thing missing was the "arrrrrrrrr".

She managed to get the knife safely away from him and from that point on, the knife block, complete with knives was relegated to the top of the fridge. A place that he never managed to climb.

On another occasion, Monica found him on the bathroom counter. As she entered the room, he had his back to her. She asked "Ant, what are you doing darling"?

He turned around to face her. He had my disposable razor in his hand and his chin and neck were covered in blood.

"Oh my God", she cried, checking her shock so as not to upset him.

He was smiling. She grabbed him and washed his face only to find a very small knick on his lip. It was a small cut but it bled a lot. But Anthony was apparently very proud that he could shave, just like his dad.

You can imagine how very frightening it was for Monica.

On another occasion, I discovered just how smart this kid was. Our back yard where we lived at the time was small but completely fenced in. Where the fence met the house on either side we had gates with the typical latch device that would (supposedly) keep kids and animals out. These latches were on the outside of the gates. Anthony was crawling around the back yard. He wasn't able to walk at that point and I took a break from reading a book and watched him for a while. He crawled up to one of the gates and pulled himself up onto his feet. He then reached his small hand through the fence and simply unlatched the lock, got back on his hands and knees and proceeded to crawl through the open gate. This kid would stop at nothing. Well, obviously I had to do something about those latches. Being a handy man of some renown, I quickly grabbed some wire and wired both latches on the gates. It would take a few years before he could unwind those things I thought.

A couple of weeks later on a lovely summer Sunday morning, I was in the kitchen sitting at the table reading the paper. This was our first home and I liked that kitchen because the table was at the street end of the house. I could look up and see through the window down the driveway to the street. It was great to see approaching visitors or passers by. I could also simply turn my head in the opposite direction (without getting up) and look through the kitchen and dining room into the back yard through the patio door.

On this particular Sunday I happened to look out the window toward the street. What I saw shocked me. There was Anthony crawling his way down the driveway toward the street on hands and knees. His little diapered bottom bobbing from side to side as if he were proud to have escaped the confines of the back yard.

I bolted for the door and grabbed him off of the driveway about 10 feet short of the street. Who was this kid, Houdini? I checked both gates and saw that the wiring was still intact. My only conclusion was that he had opened the patio door leading to the back yard and somehow climbed over the gate and crawled to the driveway.

Another thing he was getting good at was unlocking the front door and attempting a more direct escape. Once again putting my handy man skills to work, I installed a sliding bolt on the main door about 6 feet from the floor. When he got to the age where he could reach the sliding bolt, he'd be old enough to come and go as he pleased.

Life with Anthony was a constant and enjoyable game of keeping him a) contained and b) entertained.

When Monica returned to work, we had her mother look after Anthony during the weekdays. Being directly from Dublin, Ireland I called her "me Mammy" and she had a fantastic relationship with her grandson. She had been retired from a career in nursing and was happy to look after Ant for a few years. Monica and I often wondered what state her house would be in as we arrived to pick him up every day. He could be a hand full for the strongest of adults and Mammy was 110 pounds soaking wet. So he could get fresh air at his granny's house I essentially built a compound out of temporary snow fencing in her back yard. I made sure that he would be unable to climb it and for once was successful in making it escape proof.

Perhaps he just never tried to escape. One afternoon, I arrived to pick him up and saw one of the many ways his granny kept him entertained. He was in the kitchen, sheets of newspaper scattered on the floor. He loved to play with sheets of newspaper, open and on the floor. He would put his hands on them and move them quickly back and forth. I imagine he liked the sound and movement of the paper. He also loved to make noise, a lot of noise. To feed this love, granny would let him open all of the drawers in the kitchen and let him take out everything he could. He preferred pots and pans, and of course, wooden spoons. He would bang on the pots for what seemed to be hours. I still don't know how his grandmother didn't go either deaf or out of her mind with the noise.

This was the first indication of his love of playing the drums. When he was 15 he had built himself a small drum kit out of old coffee cans, using packing tape for the skins. At Christmas that year we bought him a beautiful set of drums, which he adored, and played frequently to our pleasure.

As a toddler, we found out early what kind of heart our Anthony had. His main playing area was our basement. I had made it safe enough so he could be left down there to play and watch movies. One afternoon he was in his usual play mode and we were in the kitchen keeping a keen ear for too much noise, or worse, too little noise. All was well as we could hear him chatting to his toys with some movie playing in the background. To our surprise, he came up stairs crying softly. After a quick visual inspection I saw that he hadn't injured himself in any way, so I asked.

"What's the matter Ant"?

"Fox go away".

"Pardon"?

"Fox go away", he repeated as tears rolled down his cheeks. I went downstairs to see that he was watching the movie, "The Fox and the Hound", a story about a dog that befriends a fox. Part of the story is when the farmer must banish the fox, as it is frightening animals on a neighboring farm.

All this to say that Anthony was touched emotionally by the fact that the fox was forced to leave his friend the dog. Up to that point I had not realized how sensitive my son was.

There were many days when Monica would bring Anthony to the local playground to run around and let loose. On one particular day while Monica was pregnant with Alanna, she was singing a song from the animated movie "Pocahontas". When she finished the song Anthony cupped Monica's face with both hands and said,

"Mommy, I love you like John Smith loves Pocahontas".

In the months that followed we discussed how we would proceed with his education. We did some research and were impressed with the learning format and methodology of the Montessori method of education and decided to enroll him at age two. We were very happy with the way he was treated and the simple rules the students must follow; among them was the rule that you must push your chair in when you leave the table and if you play with something you must put it back where you got it.

Each day after work Monica and I would drive to the school to pick him up. On a number of occasions I recognized a woman that I remembered from university. She had a little boy in the same class as Anthony. I would greet her with the usual "hello, how are you". One afternoon she approached Monica and me and said "thank you".

"What for", I replied?

"Your son is the only child in the class that will play with my son", she said, as tears welled up in her eyes.

"He is a special needs child", she said choking back a sob.

"When he was delivered, he was without oxygen for a short while and that affected his brain".

"And I wanted to thank you for your son being so nice to him, no one else in the class will play with him".

So, we suddenly knew that we had a very kind and sensitive little boy on our hands. We were very proud of that moment.

He was a classic example of what is called a spirited child. A spirited child is one that is described in "Raising Your Spirited Child" by Mary Sheedy Kurcinka;

*"The word that distinguishes spirited children from other children is **more**. They are normal children who are more intense, persistent, sensitive, perceptive, and uncomfortable with change than other children. All children possess these characteristics, but spirited kids possess them with a depth and range not available to other children. Spirited kids are the Super Ball in a room full of rubber balls. Other kids bounce three feet off the ground. Every bounce for a spirited child hits the ceiling".*

One classic example of this spirit and drive was the first time we took him to IKEA. IKEA stores have a great set-up for kids. You sign them in to a type of daycare where they are looked after while the parents shop. After signing him in, we shopped for about an hour, paid for our items and proceeded to sign Anto out of the daycare unit. When we arrived we were a little surprise at what was going on. In the daycare unit there is one of those classic rooms filled with the colored balls that the children can jump around in. Safe enough. In this room there was a slide next to the pile of colored balls that the children could climb and jump into the balls if they wanted to. As is the case with all slides, a ladder is connected to it for the children to get to the top of the slide.

As we approached we could see the surprised and concerned expression on the daycare workers' faces as Anthony would climb to the very top of the ladder and in what I can only imagine was an attempt at flight, fling himself as high and as far as he could into the mass of cushy balls. He would then get up, run to the ladder and do it again. Fortunately there were no other children in the room as I am sure a body slam from my son would have, at the very least terrified any victim of "The Flying Antman". When we signed him out, we could see the visible expression of relief on the caregivers' faces.

That energy and seeming absence of fear, combined with his size made him a going concern. Even before he was born I would stare at Monica's belly in amazement, as he would constantly be moving, her tummy bulging and moving in an odd manner. I couldn't help but think of the scene in the movie "Alien" just before the creature pops out of the man's stomach. Of course the monster in the movie would have been no match for the power and determination of my "Antman". He had the will of ten men, as Monica would always say.

On one Saturday afternoon, Monica and I were in the kitchen doing dishes or something when we heard a muffled bang, followed by a thud. We looked at each other and seconds later we heard it again, bang, thud!

The sound was coming from the living room and we cautiously peered around the corner to see Anthony perched on the arm of a wing-backed chair. He was naked, except for his diaper; knees bent looking intently at the wall, which was about 4 feet away from the chair. He sprang from the arm of the chair, hands and feet hitting the wall first before he would thud to the floor.

"What are you doing sweetie", Monica asked as he got up off the floor looking frustrated.

"I can't stick", he replied.

"Pardon", said a confused Monica.

"I'm Spiderman and I can't stick", he said with a frustrated whimper in his voice.

"OK, sweetie, but Spiderman is a cartoon and he has special powers so please don't try to stick to the wall anymore, OK"?

"Ok", he said. And he never, to our knowledge, tried that again.

Being big in life, so too he was big in the womb, so much so that doctors told us that because of his size, there was a chance he could be born with a mental disability. All that comment did, was put fear and panic into us. They should have kept their mouths shut without any sufficient proof of this idiotic theory.

He was bullied at school because of his size, which as one can imagine, upset him very much. His grade six teacher handled the bullies in a manner that was enviable. After a phone call from Monica to her, she dealt with the bullies without humiliating or shaming them and calmed Anthony's pain. It was a win for Anthony and a lesson for the bullies. I don't know what she said to the bullies but it worked. It was simply brilliant.

His size also made it difficult to handle him physically. It also made for some odd reactions from strangers. Because he was so big as a child, people often thought he was much older than he actually was. He was also a good-looking kid. People would see him and start speaking to him. "Hello, what a good looking little boy you are", they would say, expecting an intelligible response. When they got the jabbering of someone his age, a furrow would form on their brow. Some even said, "He has a speaking problem"?

"I'm sure he'll be OK", they would add.

My response was to say, "He's only three years old".

People consistently assumed that he was older than he actually was.

"Oh, he's so big", they would conclude.

When he was three years old, I very seriously considered having a tee shirt made for him that said,

"Give me a break. I'm only three years old"!

In fact, he had some difficulty pronouncing some things and often the pronunciation was, well, unique. One day while out for a walk along our street, a large dump truck came rumbling by. This was a great sight for Anthony to see and he shouted, "look daddy, a big dumb fuck"!!

In addition to his physical strength and enthusiasm he had a booming voice. A voice that was loud in childhood and unmistakable in adulthood. In his teen years he would be the lead singer in what he called a hard-core band. The type of music they played was a combination of screaming guitars, crashing symbols and of course Anthony's guttural, screaming voice. I photographed his debut performance at a skateboard park and was very happy to use the earplugs I kept in my camera bag. They were absolutely necessary. I don't think I will ever understand the allure of this type of music, which appealed mainly to what my wife calls "angry, angst ridden teenage boys". But when I asked some of his friends how he was doing, their unanimous response was that he was really good at it. So, at least he was doing a good job at it. He continued performing in his band, "Hostility" until his death. In fact, he had planned on leaving the band to pursue other music ventures and his last performance would have been the night after he was killed.

Speaking of his voice and how it could be very loud when he was younger, it was difficult to get into his head that in some situations he should try to keep his voice down. He seemed to not understand this and it could be embarrassing and interruptive to say the least. Monica had an idea. She sat him down one day and said,
"Anthony darling, you know how sometimes mommy and daddy say, shhh, keep your voice down"?

"Ya", he replied.

"Well, we say that because it means that at that moment we need you to be quiet. It also means that you're being a little too loud for everyone because you're such a big strong boy. So we're going to make up a secret word that means it's time to be quiet, OK"?

"OK", he replied.

"The secret word is gadzooks", she added.

"Gadzooks", he said.

And that seemed to do the trick. From that moment on, when he was getting a little too loud, simply saying the word "gadzooks" would quiet him down. You use whatever works, I guess.

It was also a challenge containing him in public places. He simply would not sit still. He wanted to do everything and go everywhere, right now! An excursion as simple as a trip to the grocery store was an exercise in tactical planning that would rival any covert military operation. Being rested, fed and a trip the bathroom prior to any venture beyond the end of the driveway was mandatory.

Tactic number 1.

I'd get to the store and carry him to the area where the shopping carts were. At this point I want to thank God and all of the people involved in the design and development of those nylon belts that clip and hold kids in those carts. They kept my Anthony secure for about three grocery store visits before he figured out how to undo the clip and try to wrestle his way out of the cart and away from Monica and me.

Tactic number 2.

At this point he was about three years of age I couldn't shop and keep him in control if he was not tied into the shopping cart, he would simply run to the furthest part of the store looking for adventure. I needed to keep him in the cart and there simply was no alternate option for that. Since he knew how to unlatch the plastic clip that held less determined children in the cart I had an idea. I took off my belt, put it around his waist, spun it around so the buckle was behind him and out of reach and voilà! Problem solved.

Then the screaming started.

He couldn't undo himself and he let everyone know how he felt about that. I think people as far away as the parking lot could hear his screams of frustration at not being able to escape the cart.

Tactic number 3.

My son had a phenomenal appetite. I suppose the appetite was needed to feed the engine of physical determination. In those days it seemed that there were always food-sampling stations spread throughout our local grocery store. In hindsight, perhaps the store manager did this to keep spirited children in check. It worked for us. There was always a person manning a food sample station handing out samples of baked beans, really tasty baked beans. Thank the Lord for Loblaw's baked bean samples is all I can say. He loved them and that would buy us a few moments of shopping without having to think ahead to plan our next covert "op" in keeping our son corralled.

There did come a time when we did allow him out of the cart to walk around. This was most effective when we would grab something like a box of rice cakes off of the shelf, rip the container open and feed him one or two in exchange for him staying close by. That tactic lasted for about two shopping trips.

Tactic number 4.

Knowing that Anthony's days sitting in the shopping cart were pretty much finished, I needed another containment method and I had just the idea.

A great spot was under the cart where shoppers place larger items such as cases of soda, etc. I convinced him (convince may be too strong a word as for this tactic, Anthony required little convincing) to lie on his stomach on the under part of the cart with his head jutting out like the carved figurehead on an old square-rigged ship. This was dangerous, as was pointed out on more than one occasion by (usually) old ladies. But I was desperate and careful. I'm happy to say that there were no incidents during the utilization of tactic number 4.

Thus, a few examples of what it is like to have to deal with a spirited child. Hard work yes, but worth every second of it. Those of you reading this who have a spirited child know of what I speak.

Along came Alanna

During this always-interesting period of strategies and tactics development, our daughter Alanna was born. Alanna Brigitte McColl was born on August 10, 1995, also close to nine pounds, but being big wouldn't last with Alanna as it did with Anthony. Alanna's curse or blessing, however you look at it was and still is beauty. When Monica announced to friends and family that she was expecting a second child, the normal response was one of shock and surprise followed by a facial expression as if to say "are you crazy? Don't you have enough to deal with in Anthony"?

Having said that, I do not recall ever having any feelings of hesitation or fear of having a second child. If anything, at this point I regret not having more children. But I digress.

In terms of pregnancy, delivery, behavior and upbringing, Alanna was pretty much the opposite of her brother. She does share his kindness, sensitivity and love of rugby.

Labor for Monica was five hours. Delivery was natural and from what I witnessed, far less painful than Anthony's delivery. My little "Beauty" was born. Our stay in hospital was less than 24 hours and while there, Monica's sister took care of our wandering escape artist, without incident. The morning of August 11, 12 hours after Alanna's birth, we saw what was to become the core of Anthony's relationship with his sister.

We were in the room with Monica and the Midwife was preparing to show us how to bathe Alanna. In walked three year old Anthony and he said with excitement, "where's my baby sister"?

"Here she is", Monica replied.

"Would you like to give her a bath", added the Midwife?

And so, Anthony gave his sister her very first bath.

Her first spoken word was mama and the second word in her vocabulary was "buvva", meaning brother.

Alanna was a beautiful child. So much so that upon seeing her, strangers in stores would buy things and give them to her. Store clerks would give her candy saying, "you're such a beautiful little girl, here's a candy for you".

To which she would respond, "I have a brother, can I have a candy for him too please"?

Whenever she was given some small treat, she would always ask for second one for her big brother.

Their relationship was set and they shared a strong, unwavering love for each other that would be envied by friends of ours that had multiple children. Most of which had difficulty getting along.

I remember being in a shopping mall a few months later with Alanna in her stroller and Anthony obediently (for a change) tagging along. It happened rarely but that day Alanna was a little cranky and she started to cry off and on. Wanting to console her I spoke to her asking the usual, "are you OK sweetie"? That didn't work.

Why not put the old Antman to work, I thought.

"Anthony", I said.

"Alanna's upset could you sing to her please"?

He immediately rushed to the side of the stroller and broke into song.

"Bah, bah bwack (black) sheep, have you any wool...", he started with a little more intensity than I thought was required, but I didn't interrupt him, he was doing something to console his sister and I certainly didn't want to quash his good intentions. It was very cute.

I also remember a few years later, we were taking Alanna to her very first dental appointment, the Antman in tow of course. In the car she was telling us how scared she was and in another attempt to offer his little sister comfort, he declared,

"Don't worry Alanna; the dentist isn't going to saw your teeth off".

It made Monica and I laugh but was little comfort to Alanna. Once Alanna was in the dentist chair she was comforted when Anthony stood next to her and held her hand during the entire examination. That, she would tell us 10 years later, gave her tremendous comfort.

In fact the night he died, Anthony was in the process of looking after his sister once again. He was to make sure that if she needed a ride home from the party she was attending, he would take his mother's car and go and get her. We had always impressed upon him the hazards of dangerous driving including driving under the influence and he was adamant in holding to that rule. One time he was at a camp with friends. They'd been drinking. All that was there was a somewhat dilapidated, uninhabitable trailer. Since there were essentially no beds in the trailer and the car seats were full, Anthony ended up sleeping in the trunk of the car. No drinking and driving.

The Crash

After many weeks of hearsay accounts of what happened and calls to the police, we finally had a chance to sit with the investigating detectives. The lead investigator was with the Surete du Quebec (SQ). The provincial force is always called in to investigate when there is a death and a local police force is involved.

April 15 was a Friday and it being a weekend and close to summer, police cars would set up on one of the many side roads dissecting highway 148. This night was no different. About three kilometers east of where the accident occurred, two officers of the MRC des Collines Police force were seated in their parked cruiser on a side road, waiting for someone to tear by so they could pursue and do the usual pull over thing. The lead SQ detective claimed in his report that the two local officers were "bored" and that they would follow the next passing car, regardless of speed.

Along came Brian Campbell in his 2002 Mazda. The officers pulled out onto highway 148 and started following Mr. Campbell's car. Campbell must have noticed the pursuing cruiser and started to increase his speed. The cruiser accelerated as well, the lights on the roof flashing red and blue. The detective said that Campbell's driving was approaching increasingly dangerous speeds and he started passing cars as he quickly approached them. After making note of the model and year of the car and recording the license plate number, the officers decided to "break off" the pursuit for safety reasons. I don't know for certain where exactly along the highway the decision was made to "break off" and I'm not thoroughly convinced that the police actually did "break off" the chase. Campbell was traveling very fast, which made the police suspect he was drunk. On a sweeping left hand curve in the road, his right front wheel drifted onto the gravel shoulder. As is all too common, he overcorrected and once the tire re-connected with the pavement, the Mazda jerked to the left, sending the car on an uncontrolled trajectory directly into the path of my son's car.

The photos of the car in the newspaper were frightening. The site of such devastation brought tears to people's eyes. Oddly enough Campbell's car was not as damaged as Anthony's. In the months that followed, I had two occasions to personally inspect the vehicles, one to recover personal belongings, purses, etc., and once, after the police were finished taking the standard crash investigation measurements. On the first occasion, I discovered that there is a standard procedure for the people cleaning up at the crash scene. While the police are at the scene of the crash they mark and record all of the necessary skid marks and bits and pieces of the vehicles on the road. This determines speed, angle of impact, etc. When the clean up crew comes along with the tow truck, it appears that they simply shovel all of the debris into the car before it is carted off to the yard where it is held for the investigators to measure what I call impact points on the cars. I believe that the depth of the impact point, which is the distance between a part of the car before it is hit and the depth of damage the car sustains after impact help determine speed. Since the roof of my son's car had to be completely removed with the Jaws of Life in order to extricate the girls, it was simply laid on top of the car completely covering all of the broken glass, car parts and dirt that filled the car up to the dashboard. On first visit we could only access the trunk where we found a few purses and my son's favorite backpack. There was no way I could access where the occupants were as it was full of sharp, oily wreckage and I had to await clearance from the police to go through it once the vehicle measurements were complete.

Weeks later, I got the call from the insurance company that the car was cleared and I could do what I wish with it. I felt compelled to go back to the car to see where my son drew his last breath. To touch this mangled wreck and wonder again if he suffered in any way. People would ask later how I could bring myself to do such a dark thing. It was difficult but I had to. The thought of doing that made me feel closer to him in some way. I arrived, put on gloves to protect myself from the shards of glass, metal and plastic and proceeded to empty the car. I wanted to find the new shoes I had bought him a week earlier but the impact was so severe that I couldn't even see the floor where his feet would have been. It was simply crushed, folded metal. There were signs of blood on the driver's seat, a lot of blood. Blood that I thought couldn't be his as his injuries were not visible when we saw his body in the hospital on that grey morning. I found out five months later that in order to extricate Lea, the girl that was sitting to Anthony's right, they first had to remove him. So the blood on the seat was hers from the terrible gash that perfectly replaced her left eyebrow. I can only imagine that her head hitting the rear view mirror caused the cut. It must be mentioned here that the girls in the car with Anthony survived only because of the words I always used to utter to everyone when they get into my car. Anthony repeated those words every time he had passengers in the car.

"Buckle up everyone"!

This too was confirmed by his passengers months later.

The detective went on to say that Mr. Campbell was not

wearing a seat belt. Crash scene investigators determined that upon impact, Campbell's head hit and broke the windshield of his car, though he didn't go through the windshield. He had hit Anthony's Honda Civic at an angle and Campbell's car spun violently down the road. The spin caused a sort of blender effect, turning Campbell around and around in the car until he was ejected through the (closed) passenger window and flung onto the gravel shoulder, on the other side of the road, a number of meters further west. He too died instantly and must have been in appalling condition.

"What would have happened if Campbell had been wearing his seatbelt", I asked the detective?

"He would have been OK", he replied quietly, with a slight grin on his face.

"Jesus Christ", was all I could mutter.

My mind raced for an instant. What if Campbell had survived, I wondered? How would I feel then?

My son dead at the hands of a man evading police.

As quickly as that thought entered my head, it disappeared and to this day I don't have that debate with myself.

Thank God I don't have that debate.

Sometimes, internal survival mechanisms really help, sometimes not so much.

"Do you have the autopsy report", I asked?

"Its not complete", he responded.

"When should we expect it"?

"Between six months and one year".

"When the police are involved and a death occurs, there is a thorough investigation conducted by the province, so it takes longer to complete", he concluded.

"You must be a busy man", I asked?

"The only thing we investigate are murders and homicides, and we are very busy".

"It must be a tough job", I said wondering how this guy can cope with all of that violent death, day in and day out.

He simply nodded and smiled.

So my son was killed and the lives of four girls changed forever by a 21 year old man that made some very bad decisions, one of which was to run from the police.

Grief

Grief is not linear. Numerous studies show that grief effects people in similar ways. Anger, shock, disbelief, denial and depression. Although these feelings affect everyone who is grieving a loss, they hit you at different times in different levels of intensity. There is no set pattern or time frame for these feelings to come along. Therefore it's very difficult to manage them when they arrive unexpectedly. Particularly at times that are inconvenient. And that is guaranteed to happen at least once during the grieving process.

Steven Jenkinson is known as the "Griefwalker". He works as a palliative care counselor at Mount Sinai Hospital in Toronto. Mr. Jenkinson works mainly with people who are dying and those relatives that are going through the process of grief. He says that grief is not a feeling, it's a skill, and the twin of grief is the love of life. I take that to mean, the more you love life, the better you will be at handling grief.

I've always loved life. I enjoy nature, history, learning new things and exploring. Perhaps that's how I am surviving this most difficult time. I have lost my first born in a terrible and preventable car crash, and this has become an opportunity for me. This is an opportunity to go down one of two roads.

The first road is one of anger, hatred and self-pity. This is a road that would be unhealthy for anyone and the people around them. It makes people miserable and will take years off of a person's life.

The second road is the opportunity to become a different and better person. I can take this tragedy and turn it into something positive. I can be positive and take good things from my situation and use those things to make the world (at least my world) a better place. "Tony's Promise" is one of those things.

I can take the high road and show my family and others that we can overcome adversity with kindness, compassion, understanding and pride.

I will not let the negative feelings of self-pity and anger draw me down to an existence of pain and misery. Although self-pity does creep into my mind often, that is when I am forced, and gladly so, to think about the "switches" in my brain and make sure that the "self-pity" switch is off and the "think positive" switch is turned on. This in no way reduces the sadness and grief I feel about the loss of my son, but it certainly makes it more bearable.

I am a sensitive man. I am appalled by violence. It pains me to see what despot leaders can do to their people and not understand the evil they commit. The sheer ridiculousness of gang violence to show how tough a person or group is angers me in its utter senselessness. I also don't like killing things for no reason, especially insects. People kill spiders because they "don't like them", I don't understand that. If you don't like spiders, stay away from them. I eat meat and believe that animals must die to feed people and other animals. It is necessary for life; in my opinion humans are not naturally vegetarians. Some choose that way of life and it's not my place to judge them regarding their choice to not eat meat. The Dalai Lama is probably the best-known vegetarian on the planet but when he suffered an illness a number of years ago, his doctor recommended he eat at least some meat to help in the healing process. It was the same case for former Blink-182 drummer Travis Barker, who was badly burned in a plane crash. He is a vegetarian but his doctor also recommended that he eat meat to heal more effectively. I'm not positive but I doubt that Travis Barker and the Dalai Lama have the same doctor.

Up until my son's death I didn't cry much and certainly not in public (there is that damn male machismo thing again). My mother died at the age of 57 after a lengthy illness. I had mourned her death in the years prior to her death but didn't realize that until much later. I was not sad when my mother died. I was relieved.

My father died of natural causes at age 84 and all of my crying for him was done at his bedside in the hospital in the days before he died. My father was a sensitive man and naturally, that is where Anthony and I got that trait. My dad was a WWII veteran, serving overseas from 1939 to 1945. I'm not entirely sure if he ever made it back to Canada for breaks in between those years but I'm told he witnessed some pretty disturbing stuff. He never spoke of the bad things, like a lot of veterans, he held those things in, he spoke occasionally of the good times like running into his identical twin brother (and my favorite uncle) Harold in various places during the war. A family member had also told me that my father was affected by what he saw in the war (as I'm sure everyone who was there was affected in some way). When he returned to Canada he took up residence with an aunt. An Aunt with what I'm told had a notorious mean, unpleasant streak. Other than that, I know nothing of his war experiences. I do remember my father having a terrible stutter, not caused by his experiences during the war but from a very young age. His stutter occasionally brought impatience out in some people. My dad, a kind and gentle man would sometimes be told, "hurry up" and "say what you have to say", by ignorant and intolerant bastards! At the time, we were living close to a military base in Ottawa. It was around 1965, toward the end of the Cold War. One particular day we were on our way to visit my uncle Harold who worked on the base. The routine, as some of you may recall in those days, was to stop at the guardhouse of all Canadian military installations and give your name to the guard before being allowed to enter the grounds. We did this regularly and on this day, the same guard we saw every time we visited the base was on duty. The guard would say. "What's your name please"?

My dad would respond, "Gordon M, M, M, Mc, Mc, Mc, Coll". On this particular day, half way through my father's stuttering, the guard interrupted and said, "Hurry up, what's your name"?

On that day, I got impatient for a change and shouted, "McColl, Gordon McColl" and spelled it, "M-C-C-O-L-L, OK"? I must have been about 10 years old.

I also remember that over time, my father lost his stutter. I don't how or why that happened.

As mentioned earlier about my then young Anthony coming up stairs crying while watching the movie The Fox and the Hound. I recall very vividly as I watched Anthony do that. It brought me back to my childhood. One day, when I was young, my father had walked up to the corner store to purchase milk or something like that. When he returned, he came into the house with tears running down his face. My mother asked him what was wrong. He had apparently encountered a young boy afflicted with Polio. The boy was walking with crutches and leg braces. This brought my father to tears.

That was the only time I ever saw him cry.

Remember, men aren't supposed to cry.

I have shed many tears since my son's death and I am not afraid to do that. I have been interviewed by the media many times since the accident and during each and every one of them I got choked up to the point where I couldn't speak. Some people can speak while choking back tears but I can't. My voice gets shaky and high pitched and no one can understand what I say. It sounds quite silly. So, to handle this, I simply pause, collect myself and continue when I am able to speak legibly. I feel compelled to continue the interview because I have things to say about how wonderful my son was and to spread the message of the Tony's Promise campaign.

As for crying, it is mixed for me. I don't mind when I get choked up on national television. It's human nature for people, including men to cry. What I have done many times since my son's death, but not in public, is all out sobbing. I save that for times when I am alone. I call those my moments of personal hell. Moments when I can no longer handle the size and weight of the anvil growing in my chest, the tears and the sobs come pouring out of me.

I must admit that the ridiculous notion of men not being allowed to cry still lingers within me. I get pangs of embarrassment after a good "blub". But when a parent has lost a child it is very therapeutic to cry in fits and sobs. The tears burning in my eyes, the release of the anvil's weight in my chest, the freedom of feeling and the knowledge that I will not succumb to my grief. My body and my mind giving me the ability to purge the pain and tumult of grief. I feel that I've given myself permission to cry, and that's a good thing. When I cry, I win. My grief does not.

Usually I will feel the grief building inside me. The anvil I mentioned earlier. As time goes by, the anvil gets smaller and it's weight gets lighter. Grief looses its power. Never the less, the anvil is there and I know it will remain there for a long time, perhaps never leaving completely. Normally I can feel the grief slowly growing inside me and in the days and weeks after the accident I could easily identify what was causing the episodes of intensified grief. It grows in my chest like a cumulous cloud growing bigger and darker, becoming the storm that would undoubtedly explode in a deluge of rain. Of course the rain I produce is a storm of tears and the all too well known chest heaving that comes with uncontrollable sobbing.

In the first ten months after the crash, I could easily recognize the advance signals starting as the monthly anniversary date approached. In the days approaching the 16th of each month the anvil would start growing again and my shoulders would start to droop.

Music can jump start grief as well. When I hear a song or a style of music that reminds me of my son, I feel what I can only describe as sudden, short heaves in my chest, gasping for a breath.

I pity the man that doesn't possess the capability or knowledge and strength to show and be able to deal with grief. These flashes of grief caused by quick triggers like music or a certain smell are very difficult and sometimes impossible to quell. The floodgates will open and the storm of tears will begin. And it can happen if you are alone, on a bus or in a board meeting with your colleagues watching you fall completely apart. If you think you can control it, think again.

Fortunately, thanks to my lovely wife who is of French and Irish extraction, the ability to show and deal with grief has been pounded into my psyche over the years.

I will attempt to explain my experience of grief, and how I dealt with it from a chronological perspective.

In the days immediately following my son's death, my experience of grief was a swirling mix of sadness, shock, confusion and disbelief. All of this was jolted and displaced by the "onslaught" as mentioned earlier.

At the hospital, my experience was predominantly one of shock and disbelief. Thinking back on that, now that I have at least some control of my feelings, I can say that a sort of energy barrier seemed to float around me. One could even call it a fog. Leaving the hospital I felt the beginnings of the anvil forming. I was torn between my practical nature, trying to maintain some control and the confusion of my Anthony being dead, all the while trying to make sure my wife and daughter were looked after. I remember driving my car home with my friend Gerry and his family following. I was being practical at that point. Drive the damn car and concentrate on that. There will be plenty of time to think about Anto when I get home... Anto... a flash went through my mind. The memory of seeing him dead on the gurney. The trickle of blood slowly flowing from his nose and the corner of his mouth. It was the same as the typical movie scene where the nurse peels back the sheet that covers the deceased and the parent identifies the body. I know what you people who are reading this are now saying to yourselves, "I can't imagine". You probably even say this when you see it on television or in a movie. Well, I hope you never get that dreadful opportunity.

That scene conjures up images that I see each and every time I think of my son. The first image of him is the following photograph and the second is of him on that gurney with the blood on his face and his eyes slightly open and staring at something over my left shoulder.

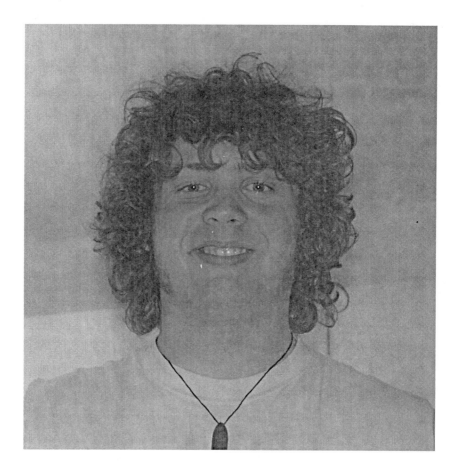

This mental vision has a thought process connected to it as well. I see the "photo" of him in my mind and I think of how handsome he was. I think of his size, his kind heart, his booming voice and his infectious laugh. Sometimes I can even smell him and recall how it felt to hug him and hold his massive hand. Then it switches to the vision of him on the gurney and I see him in death, pale and lifeless but still good looking, oddly enough. Then I sense his smell in the hospital, his usual scent tainted with blood and other bodily fluids, not repulsive but certainly not the scent he emitted in life.

In the days, weeks and months that followed I began to experience what would become what I call the "rollercoaster". A good analogy I believe, that compares the exaggerated peaks and valleys of grief, the most positive of which is a neutral and numb feeling. The worst of which is thinking that I may quite simply go out of my mind with sadness, the almost unbearable feeling of loss through missing him.

The first night, Saturday, April 16, the end of the first day of the onslaught, we sat in our kitchen, alone. Alanna went to a friend's house for the night and I think the distraction was good for her.

We live in our kitchen. There is a flat screen television on an interior wall and, looking to the left there is an exterior wall with three narrow, tall windows that look out to our street. These windows look out the street but do not offer a view of the driveway, so with the outside lights on, anyone approaching would suddenly appear through these windows as they came to our front door.

When Anthony was alive, returning home at night, as he approached the house he would suddenly appear, walking by the windows to the entrance. We would see him flash by, sometimes startling us, but it was always a welcome sight. My son was home, safe and unharmed. On that first night, I kept looking, looking in the desperate hope that he would flash by those windows and come into the house. Each night following the accident, I would leave the outside lights on in case, by some incredible miracle, he did come home. But that was not to be, and after about a week, with difficulty and tears in my eyes, I turned the outside lights off before going to bed. One small but significant step in accepting that he was dead and would not return. At least not physically.

Earlier that day during a lull in the almost constant bombardment of well-wishers, I went into our basement. Our house is essentially square and the basement is divided equally by the stairs. At the bottom of the stairs to the basement you can turn right 180 degrees and enter Anthony's side, which is his bedroom. Turn left and you enter the television and laundry rooms.

As I approached the bottom of the basement stairs, I noticed a tea towel on the floor. It is customary in my house that if there is a dirty tea towel in the kitchen, simply toss it down the stairs and on your next trip down there, grab the towel and bring it to the laundry room. I reached the bottom of the stairs and as I picked up the towel, I realized that someone else was in the basement. Another person was there. I immediately thought that Monica had come down to Anthony's bedroom to sit at his desk and go through some of his belongings. Now keep in mind that his desk is hidden from view when at the bottom of the stairs. You basically have to turn 180 degrees to your right when you reach the basement, walk about eight paces and only as you approach the back of the room do you see his desk and anyone who may be sitting at it. I turned, fully expecting to see Monica sitting there because I knew someone was in that room. I'm sure people who have experienced this know what I mean. You can feel a person's presence, most of the time. I was somewhat shocked when in the poorly lit room I saw the chair empty and no one in the room. Then I saw a flash of something I will never forget. There on the far side of the bed, wearing his favorite sleeveless undershirt and his hair, long and wavy, was my son.

He was just standing there looking at me. I couldn't make out his facial expression, it was more like his silhouette surrounded by a beautiful blue glow. The blue glow that I have since read about in so many books on death and near death experiences.

In an instant he was gone. In fact I didn't know what I was looking at until after he vanished. It took a few minutes as I ascended the stairs to the kitchen and I realized that I had seen the spirit of my son. My God, he was there. Why did he not stay longer? Why didn't he say something to me? I have not seen him since but he seems to leave a lot of signs that he is thinking about us. I replay that moment over and over in my memory and if I ever get to where he is now, the first thing I will say to him is, "I saw you when you came to your bedroom that morning, thank you for that".

On another occasion, I was in his room looking down at the floor, I noticed three coins between his bed and his desk. Nothing odd there, his room was usually messy and cluttered. I picked up the coins and put them in my pocket thinking nothing of the find. A day later I'm in his room once again. Oddly enough in pretty much the same place I see three more coins on the floor. They were out in the open, how could I have missed them the day before?

I picked those up as well and keep them on his desk.

A week or so later I was chatting on the phone with my friend Laurie who is a sort of clairvoyant. She claims that she can see energy from people who have passed and are trying to communicate with the living. This is something I'm not really sure I believe in and take what she says with a grain of salt. She is a very good friend nonetheless. I mentioned the coin discovery to her and she simply said.

"Oh yes, that's common when angels want to let you know that they are thinking of you. They'll leave coins or feathers, usually three at a time. Sometimes just one coin or one feather."

At that point I thought of using more than just one grain of salt. But something happened that made me wonder.

I few weeks later I was at the bank. I approached the teller to conduct my transaction and I was surprised at what I saw. On the counter, clearly visible to the teller and me were three coins, two pennies and a nickel. Now, finding coins on the floor in my son's still messy bedroom (or on the street for that matter) is very self-explanatory. People drop coins all the time. But seeing three coins on the counter in front of a bank teller is odd. Why in a bank of all places would coins just be left on the counter and not taken by the teller or the customer? It made me think of my son playing a joke on me from Heaven.

My sister told me she has seen him on two separate occasions, as big as life. The first time she saw Anthony was when she went grocery shopping a few months after his death. The store she visited was connected to a string of stores in a strip mall. As she walked from the store through the parking lot to her car, she passed by a Home Depot store. She looked up and sitting on the roof of the Home Depot, there he was looking down at her. He was dressed in his usual clothing, baggy shorts and a tee shirt. The only difference, she said was that he had large, white angel wings on his back.

"Hey Auntie Jodan" (her name is really Joanne but as a child he could only say "Jodan" and that name stuck).

"Can I have a piece of that orange cake", He asked?

"Sure", she replied, and he was gone.

Oddly enough, she was carrying an orange cake that she had purchased at the grocery store.

The second time she saw him was when she was on a city bus on the way into work one morning. The bus was in downtown Ottawa, nearing her stop she noticed that Anthony was sitting at the very top and on the corner of a twenty-story office tower. Tee shirt, shorts and, of course, the wings. He didn't see her, she says, he was just looking out over the city and looking very content.

A few weeks after the accident I was contacted by my employer. I was working on a contract in the federal government and was down to working on an as required basis, meaning part time. There were a few weeks of work available and if I felt up to it, I could come in and do some work. I needed the money and accepted. It was nice to see my colleagues again as I had been away for about two weeks. They were understandably sensitive and very supportive. I settled in and continued on with a project that I had been working on earlier in the year. Although the distraction was helpful, looking back, I don't think I was ready for work at that time. I would perform my work without any problems. The work involved conducting web based training sessions to people across the country. How I maintained my composure was surprising but I enjoy public speaking and doing presentations, so I guess I was "performing" and that was just fine. I was "normal" again, however brief it was. The days were not too bad but on approaching the noon hour each day I could feel the anvil growing, perhaps fatigue was adding to the sadness. After my morning training sessions would finish, I'd finish the paper work, etc. and after preparing everything for the afternoon session, I would go out for a walk. It became a pattern. Each day I would leave my office building located in downtown Ottawa. I would walk up to Parliament Hill. It is a beautiful historic site that is enjoyable to walk around. I would approach from the west, wander up around Center Block, where the Peace Tower is and enjoy the spectacular view of the Ottawa River and the hills of Quebec. All the while slouching from the weight if the anvil and missing my son with an uncontrollable intensity. Rain or shine I would repeat the same route each working day. I'd continue around the back of Center Block, skirt around the East Block and back to the office, eyes stinging from my tears.

Grief is something you simply must endure and try to navigate without either going insane or doing something drastic. In the weeks and months following the accident I often thought, "it doesn't matter if I live or die, life is not fair, it makes no sense and who gives a dam anyway. Why work so hard raising a wonderful, kind and loving young man when he is erased from this earth in a second". I remember hearing those words as I thought them in my head on more than one occasion. I quickly decided that those thoughts were generated by self-pity and not healthy, positive thoughts. Although that doesn't completely stop them from popping into my head from time to time.

I had recently read an interesting book on belief systems called "BrainShift" that was written by a friend of mine, Dr. Jeff Wilson. It discusses a basic and simple process. BrainShift essentially states that our internal decision processes are set to certain "defaults" through learned beliefs. By default I mean a person's automatic reaction to something. BrainShift says that we can control our default switches through conscious thinking about our default settings. We can turn our default switches off and turn on a different switch.

Say, for example that you are driving down the street and another car quickly cuts in front of you making you hit the brakes. What is your instant, automatic reaction? Someone with tendencies toward "road rage" would automatically start beeping the horn and yelling, perhaps even going after the offender with violent intentions. Road rage is, in this case, that person's default switch. By learning to think for just a split second prior to your default kicking in, this person can decide to change the switch to something else. Instead of going directly to road rage, a very quick check of what switch is going to be selected, the person could think, "it's not worth going after some idiot driver. I might lose my temper, punch the guy and then where would I be? I could accidentally kill him or he could fight back and I could get hurt."

When I get these moments of self-pity I often think of

BrainShift and manually select the switch I want. I need to be wary of my switches and how they are set and can't afford a default that is negative and self-destructive. This process has helped me get through the worst of my grief.

I will not let the negative feelings of self-pity and anger draw me into an existence of pain and misery. Although self-pity does creep into my mind often, that is where I am forced, and gladly so, to think about those switches in my brain and make sure the "self-pity" switch is off and the "think positive" switch is turned on. This in no way reduces the sadness and grief I often feel about the loss of my son but it certainly makes it more bearable. Thank you Jeff Wilson".

It's two weeks since the accident and my daughter and I are grocery shopping at our local supermarket.
"Dad, have you noticed that people are staring at us", she asks?
"Yes".
"People in here stare at us wherever we go", I add.
"Why", she asks?
"Well, they are looking at us in disbelief. First of all, they see us as having lost a child and your brother, and they can't imagine how painful it is. Secondly, they wonder how can someone who lost a child be doing a normal thing like

shopping. Shouldn't they be at home laying on the floor and sobbing uncontrollably"?

"They saw us in the newspaper and on television over and over. They saw 600 people at the funeral and how many friends came to pay their respects and they simply can't imagine what we are going through.

"Well I don't like it, are they stupid", she blurted?

"They just don't understand and really don't know what we're going through. We have to be nice and not be angry, it's difficult for them as well, I imagine", I offered, hoping that I was right.

The staring went on for weeks. I'd go out for a drink to a local establishment with friends in the weeks that followed and would see tables of other patrons, some I knew, others I didn't. Every few minutes a head would turn in my direction and look at me. I guess they were looking to see if I would break down into fits in front of them, some I would guess surprised at how I was doing something that "normal" people do.

One evening, I was on the patio at a restaurant having a bite to eat with a couple of very close friends. Since the crash, they would call us at home with regularity to see how we were getting on. At the slightest hint of our needing comforting, they would offer to come over or have us visit them. To this day they still "look after us" with kindness that we are so deeply grateful for. As for the restaurant, we were in good spirits for a couple that had lost their son a few months earlier, and of course there was the odd stare directed our way. At one point our friend Rick said something very funny and the four of us burst into laughter. Well the stares were a little more intense at that moment. Even people we were acquainted with looked at us as if to be saying, "Don't you realize your son is dead? How can you laugh after such a tragedy"?

To quote Christopher Reeves, after he became completely paralyzed in a riding accident, "If I can laugh, I can live".

People grieve differently and most men in my opinion grieve very poorly. It seems to be difficult for middle-aged men to grieve properly, if at all. On many occasions since the crash I was approached by a lot of friends and acquaintances. Many of them, mostly the ones that know me casually would approach, shake my hand and say, "I'm very sorry for your loss".

I would think they did this out of a feeling of obligation more than anything else. Their hands would be moist with nervous sweat and the handshake would be firm and quick. Most times there would be a slight change in their voice and their discomfort with the entire situation was abundantly clear. They wanted to offer their condolences and then get the heck away from me as soon as possible. It was odd to me and after a few of these uncomfortable moments I would offer, "If you have any questions about the accident, don't worry, I'm very comfortable talking about any aspect of it". Those words only increased the tension of the situation. I would only offer that when it seemed as if they wanted to discuss it but were afraid of upsetting me. On one particular occasion I was approached by an acquaintance, he is a manager for an organization I volunteer for and he didn't expect to see me so soon after the accident (it was about a month later). His daughter knew my son but I didn't know that at the time. He came up to me, very uncomfortable looking and said, "I'm sorry for your loss. I'm glad to see you here but I'm surprised you're here.

"Thank you", I said.

Then he seemed to catch himself and looking even more uncomfortable he said, "I'm sorry, I didn't want to remind you".

I looked at him and said, "Don't worry, I don't think I'll ever forget. It's OK. Thank you".

I decided to shut up because I didn't want to make him any more uncomfortable. He is a very kind man and I think he has a difficult time handling grief.

Monica, Alanna and I realized that after a point in time, even during the "onslaught" we would end up consoling people. On the second day of the onslaught and the constant barrage of lasagna bearing well-wishers, a pattern began. People would show up, hand me a container of food big enough to feed an Amish barn building team, give me a hug in tears, and offer their condolences. It was so kind of them and one particular friend whose son was a good friend of Anto came in. He hugged me and looked at me in tears and said, "I don't know what to say, I'm sorry".

I looked him in the eyes, I was not crying at the time and said, "It's OK John, it's OK".

Looking at me in bewilderment I think he was a little ticked and said, "No, it's not OK".

All I could respond with, as I hugged him back was, "It's OK". I simply didn't know what else to say. I was very tired.

When someone suffers the loss of a loved one, particularly a child, one of the questions you ask yourself is "where are they, in heaven? Does heaven even exist? Will I ever see him/her again"?

About a month after the loss of our son, my wife had a dream. In the dream, she was standing face to face with him. She claimed that she could hug him and smell him and that it was a great relief for her. She said he seemed giddy, like he had been drinking. He was chuckling and seemed very happy. She looked at him and said, "Are you drunk"?

"No", he replied. And then he went on to say, "mom, it's so beautiful, it's so beautiful".

Because of that dream, she is convinced and happy that he is in heaven. I feel the same way.

A few weeks later, I too had a dream about my son. In my dream we stood facing each other, Anthony not making eye contact with me but looking slightly over my head. Again, he was dressed in his old white undershirt, shorts and his hair was long and wavy.

In this dream, I could smell him and I hugged him also. It was euphoric; I was with my son again. He didn't hug back though, and I looked at him and said.

"Are you dead"?

He nodded slightly and said, "uh huh".

"Will I see you again", I asked him.

His response was "yup", and I woke up.

I took that as meaning I would see him in heaven when I die. To this day, I remember that dream vividly with a mix of happiness at being able to hug him again and sadness at the fact that it will be a while before we are together again.

I have dreamed about him a number of times since then and I

categorize my "Anthony dreams" in two ways. He is either present in my dreams or he comes to me in my dreams. The first time, described above and a second time that was a little odd. In my second dream I am laying on the floor curled up in the fetal position, Anthony appears, I do not move. He comes over to me, crouches down and completely envelopes me with his arms, his face close to mine. In my ear he whispers, "You have to let me in".

I never understood what that meant. Perhaps if I open up in some way, I will dream about him more.

In the second category, where he is present in my dreams, I don't speak with him or touch him, I simply see him. For example, in one dream I am in a classroom in his former high school. The class is full of people and we are all seated at desks facing the front. I look about five rows over and Anthony is sitting at one of the desks. He looks over at me, waves and goes back to whatever he is writing. I wake up.

In the few other dreams where he is present, he is with some of his old friends and just hanging out with them, and I see him from a distance. He doesn't notice me.

Two days after the accident, my wife woke up at about 5AM. I woke up as well and she said, "I have to go and sleep in his bed".

So she got up and with me following, we went to the basement where his bedroom is and crawled into his bed. It had a pile of his clothes on it, typical teenager's bedroom, clothes strewn everywhere. Lying there, we again could smell him as he had slept there just three nights previous, tears flowing as we both fell off to sleep. We both woke up about an hour later, lying there and looking around.

Our basement is finished with hardwood floors etc., except for the ceiling. The ceiling is open and you can see the joists with decorative wooden beams that make it look a little better that a plain unfinished ceiling. As we lay there, Monica noticed a shoebox sitting on one of the decorative beams.

"What's that", she asked.

"I'll get it".

Standing on the bed, I grabbed the box from its perch.

I sat down and we huddled together looking at the unopened box with some hesitation, as written in marker on the top of the box are the words "FUCK OFF".

"What the hell are we going to find inside this thing"?

"Open it", Monica said.

I proceeded to open the box. To our great relief it was filled with little mementos he had collected over the years. A Zippo lighter, a watch that we had bought for him a few years back, his Swiss Army Knife, little things that meant a lot to him. Nothing untoward.

In the bottom of the box was a folded up piece of paper. It was a piece of drawing paper. Anthony loved art and was in fact enrolled in the Visual Arts program at school, so we were used to seeing his room cluttered with sketches and various pieces of art.

I unfolded the paper and saw that it was what I would call a cartoon type drawing. It had four frames. In the first frame was a car coming from left to right. He was a good artist, our Anto. The first frame showed a small, red, four-door car that was clearly moving in the drawing, as he had drawn wisps on the car to imply motion.

In the second frame, the entire car is shown, still speeding along the road.

In the third frame, the car is exiting the frame on the right hand side with the wisps still indicating motion.

In the fourth frame, the car has hit a brick wall; it's broken in half and in flames.

My son was killed in a red, four door, Honda Civic and the only difference between the drawing and his actual accident are that the car Anthony was driving was hit by another car and there was no fire.

After looking at this drawing for a moment, I looked at Monica and we both said, "Holy shit"!

There was no date on the drawing, just his signature. Our guess is that it was drawn about 2005-6.

I believe that the grief process is easier to deal with if the person grieving has a certain level of emotional maturity. I have been connected to a number of tragic deaths since my son's accident and observed and even helped some people in dealing with their grief. The earliest tragedy was six months after Anthony's death. A friend of mine, and his wife were walking home from their son's house after visiting their grandson. They were walking through a grocery store parking lot. It was October 2011 and as they walked by the store they saw two young men vandalizing a display of Halloween pumpkins. Nothing too drastic, just a couple of punks destroying an outside store display after the store had closed. My friend yelled out to them, "Guys what are you doing"? Well, that brought a deluge of profanity from the vandals including foul language directed at my friend's wife. This led my friend to tell the young man not to speak to his wife like that. Suddenly one of the punks approached my friend and head butted him and down he went, hitting his head on the pavement. After going into convulsions, he went into a coma and died a week later. My friend had been retired for about a year at that point and his wife retired a month before that day. They had just returned from their "retirement vacation" in Hawaii the day before. Now because of a big-mouthed punk, a women looking forward to retirement and raising her first grandchild is a widow. Alone. We don't see each other much and when I think about her story I can't imagine what it would be like going home every night to an empty house.

I'm not sure how she is handling her grief but it can't be easy. It is still difficult for her son, the father of her grandchild.

It is the week before what would have been Anthony's twentieth birthday. Followed by the first anniversary of the crash and his burial, I feel a tremendous amount of sadness building in me. We put off burying his remains (ashes).

Grief and Surviving Children

The struggle with grief after the loss of a child is compounded when you have other children, particularly young children. With the mix of shock, pain, disbelief, sadness and all of the harsh and confusing feelings after losing a child, you still have to be on "watch" for your remaining children. It's important to monitor their feelings and actions. You must watch out for signs of depression. There are thousands of tests available on the Internet that you can conduct to determine levels of depression. I strongly advise that people look up some of these tests and test all family members for depression. The higher the score, the more quickly you should call your family doctor and get referred to someone who can help. This is a very serious matter.

This aspect of my journey through grief was one of extremely mixed feelings. I wanted to make sure Alanna was allowed to do the things that bring her comfort in her grief, but I needed to ensure she wasn't engaging in self destructive behavior. It's a delicate balancing act for a non-professional. You must get help for this, professional help. This can't be overstated. It turns out that Alanna's initial grief counselor expressed some opinions that Monica and I disagree with. Kids these days all want tattoos. Alanna is no different. During one of her counseling sessions, Alanna mentioned that she wanted to get her brother's name tattooed on her side. I don't know exactly what the counselor said but Alanna's interpretation was that it was OK to get a tattoo.

"My counselor said it was OK if I got a tattoo of Anthony's name"

Upon hearing this bit of information, my immediate response was,

"Why do you want to get that tattooed on your body, do you think you're going to forget his name"?

"No", she replied.

"The rule in this house has always been and always will be, no tattoos, period"

Why wouldn't the counselor bring that to Monica and me before giving any impression that a tattoo was OK? We decided not to address this with the counselor and never returned.

It's very difficult but also very important to make sure you are watching what your surviving children are doing. Not only do you have to be aware of your personal feelings and tend to your own needs, you also have to watch your kids. The balance of giving them what they want and what they need is tricky. My worry was that if I'm too hard on her, she would become suicidal. If I weren't hard enough, she'd run off and do other self-destructive things, away from my watchful eye.

This process is again compounded if there are extenuating circumstances. Circumstances like ours. Anthony was at that party solely to protect his sister and make sure she got home safely. Instead, he and another young man died and four young women were seriously injured. Alanna's survivor guilt must be deep and powerful and she hides it well. Too well, in fact. This is also complicated by the fact that she (at the writing of this book) is sixteen years old. The rebel age. Sixteen year olds want more freedom, most of them hate school, and no one understands them and their parents are "idiots". Couple all of this together and you've got a kid that's in a lot of pain. Time will tell how well we did as grieving parents juggling our feelings while looking out for our daughter. It has certainly taken years off of my life.

Another thing to consider is addressing un-reconciled differences with your children (or any family member for that matter). I am very lucky in that there were no outstanding differences between my son and me. Anthony was a stickler for fixing any differences in the family. Of course he and I had differences, he was a teenager after all.

The dread locks, tattoos, piercings etc., but as parents, we stuck to our guns and didn't cave in on any of those issues. If there were any issues between he and I or Monica, he would storm off mumbling curse words under his breathe, like most teenagers. It wasn't long before he would come back (usually to his mother) and put the issue on the table and sort it out. He would take much longer with me, sometimes reconciling with me through his mother. That was OK, I would feel physically ill those times we were upset with each other.

My advice is no matter what is happening in your life, you should make every attempt to reconcile any differences you have with your loved ones. Can you imagine how I would feel today if Anthony and I had any un-reconciled issues? No one needs that extra pain.

Do yourself a big favor, make a habit of getting your family together at a minimum once a week and have dinner. All sitting at the same table at the same time. No TV, no phones, no computers, no "I have to go and meet my friends", no distractions at all. Just sit together and have dinner. Talk to each other. Find out about each other's lives. If the issues are too volatile and you can't reconcile your family differences together, get assistance from someone who can help you.

Life is fleeting and you never know if and when tragedy will strike.

Now, every time Alanna is about to walk out the door to go to a friends house for a sleepover, I look at her and think, "is this the last time I will see her alive?
Will the next time I see her be in a hospital where she is laying lifeless on a gurney covered with a yellow plastic sheet"?
That thought causes me to jump out of my chair and grab her before she walks out the door. I give her a big hug and I kiss her on the cheek. I move back a bit and take in her beauty, knowing that I can't protect her from everything. I want to take all of her pain and deal with it myself but that is impossible. I don't tell her why I do this but I'm sure she knows.

Tony's Promise

www.tonyspromise.org

How it started.

As mentioned earlier, my daughter Alanna and some of her friends left the party on the night of the accident just moments before Anthony. As they were on their way home in the taxi, one of them, Richard Beard saw the police in pursuit of Brian Campbell. Richard thought little of it until early the next morning when he heard about Anthony's death. Richard knew my son and, as expected was extremely upset. The story was that Campbell was drunk but in fact, at the time of the chase, Campbell was "suspected" of being drunk. At the time of writing this, I still have no confirmation of whether Campbell had been drinking or not. In Quebec, if a death occurs related to a police chase the investigation moves up the chain to the provincial police. Once the investigation is complete, the report is given to a legal official for review. Apparently the official is supposed to determine if the police involved in the chase are responsible for the death in any way. I haven't confirmed this either.

Richard thought, "we've got to do something, we can't just sit around and let Tony's death go without notice. We need to start something; we need a cause to stop this from happening again. What a waste of a good life. Whatever we do it must be connected with Tony so people who find out about this tragedy will remember that they've got to make the right choices and not drink and drive".

"We'll call it Tony's Promise", he said.

"It will be a promise to never drink and drive"

And the pledge became;

"I promise to never get behind the wheel or let a friend get behind the wheel of a vehicle under the influence of drugs or alcohol".

Because of the fact that, at the time we didn't have confirmation that Campbell was indeed drunk, I felt it necessary to add both drugs and alcohol to the "Promise". Having both in the Promise would only add value anyway. Besides, Campbell's family had called the local Ottawa newspaper and complained that they "were being vilified by friends and family because of the media stories claiming that their son was drunk". After double-checking all of the stories in the media, I confirmed that all of them clearly stated that Campbell was a "suspected" drunk driver. None-the-less, the label stuck.

Instantly, Tony's Promise went viral. Monica and I didn't even know about it until two days later. The Monday following the accident became "Wear White for Tony" day at D'Arcy McGee High School. D'Arcy is Alanna's school and Tony's former high school.

Everyone at the school wore white tee shirts with "I Promise" printed on them. Alanna wanted to show solidarity with her friends and insisted on attending school that day. George Singfield, the school principal called me at home that same day asking if it was OK if some of the students spoke about Anthony to the throngs of reporters that showed up. I have known George since Anthony started Junior High School, he coached Anthony's football team for 4 years and I said, "by all means, speak to the media".

George also asked if we were comfortable with him speaking about the "Tony's Promise" campaign that Richard had started. I said, "Hold on for a second", I looked at Monica and said, "Do you know anything about something called the Tony's Promise campaign"?

"The what"?

"George says that Richard Beard has started something called Tony's Promise to promote anti drinking and driving and the media want the kids to talk about it".

"Sure", was her reply.

That was the first that Monica and I had heard of the campaign. George quickly explained it to us, and I said, "No problem if it can save lives, say as much as you want".

Richard and his friends created a Tony's Promise group on Face Book and, for a while, we had one thousand members signing up each day. The group peaked at just over seven thousand with people from as far away as Mexico, Czechoslovakia and France. By joining the group, you take the pledge and keep it. The group is still going strong.

This was my first taste of the power of social media and it was awe inspiring, all of this international attention because of my son's tragic death.

The following day, Alanna had decided that she needed more time at home and it was too soon to return to school on a regular basis.

I went to work quickly to give "Tony's Promise" some legs. People started to ask, "How can we help, we want to donate to Tony's Promise".

Up to that point, I had received about $3,000 in cheques and cash that I kept in a zip lock bag in my sock drawer, so setting up a bank account would be a good start.

I have seen it many times on the news, "John Doe's house burned down, the family has set up a fund where you can donate money to support the family, simply go to ABC Bank and make a donation to 'The John Doe Support Campaign'.

I live within walking distance of four banks; I'll just run over, set up an account, deposit the money and direct everyone to do the same.

After visiting two separate banking institutions, whose names shall remain undisclosed, I was getting a little frustrated.

I would ask to see the manager.

"I'd like to set up an account for my son who was killed in a car accident a few weeks ago. I want people to be able to walk in and make a donation to that account at any branch of your institution, anywhere in the world".

The response was the same at both banks. "You can't do that".

"Well what about the 'John Doe Support Campaign' I saw on television, I want an account like that", I asked.

"Oh, that's a Community Account, it's only good for one individual branch".

"Well, on the television, they said to drop by any branch of your bank to make a deposit. I have people from countries all over the world wanting to make donations. They can't just come here to make a deposit".

"The people on television made a mistake. You can't do that."

"Thank you", I said as I stormed out.

The third bank, the one that holds my mortgage and my business account said, "Of course we can do that for you".

"I want to be clear. I want people anywhere in the world where a branch of your bank exists to be able to walk into the branch and say 'I want to make a donation to Tony's Promise', without any problems".

I should have recognized the confused look in the manager's eyes when he said "OK".

We set up the account, with some trouble. I needed another person as a co-signer on the account. I called my close friend Rick and he had no problem signing.

After two weeks of waiting for the regional manager in some distant city to approve the account, it was complete, or so I thought.

I strode happily into the bank with my hand full of cheques ready for deposit.

I got to the teller, handed him the cheques that were made out to Tony's Promise and he said, "I can't deposit these. They have the wrong name on them".

"What"!?

"These cheques need to have the names David McColl and Richard Henderson on them.

"But I want the people making the donation to know that the money is going to Tony's Promise and not me"!

"We can't do that on this account", was the teller's response.

I took the cheques and left.

Bank number three was more promising. After I told them what I wanted donors to be able to do, they said no problem. I sat for about an hour filling out forms with the manager and the assistant manager. Once the forms were complete, I went to the teller to get my deposit slips. The two tellers recognized me and, after offering their condolences started to cry as their children knew my son.

I didn't have the cheques with me so with deposit slips in hand I left the bank. The next day I went back to the bank with the cheques and went to the teller. Same problem. The teller said, "We can't deposit these".

"I need to see the manager right now", I said with gritted teeth.

"The manager is out for lunch".

"Then I want to see the assistant manager".

I was led into the assistant manager's office and I explained the situation once again... "I said I wanted anyone in the world to be able to go into one of your branches and make a deposit to Tony's Promise and you said this account would allow that".

"Well, you can't do that with this account".

"Was I not clear enough"?

"I'm sorry you can't do that with this type of account".

"I'll wait for the manager". The branch manager was "on lunch", but I could see her in her office. She wasn't eating anything, just sitting there.

Finally, the manager, looking smug asked me into her office.

"What's the problem", she said.

"You told me I could have an account where anyone in the world with a local branch of your bank could accept deposits to Tony's Promise".

"I'm sorry, we can't do that".

"Then why did you say you could"?

"Because you were in a hurry".

"I never said that I was in a hurry when I set up this account".

"Don't raise your voice at me". She responded.

"Madam, this is not an account for a little league baseball team. This is an account for the memory of my dead son". I replied with tears filling my eyes.

I was beside myself with anger.

"I'm sorry, we can't help you".

"I am telling you right now, someone at head office is going to hear about this", I said in disgust.

Then another thing happened that astonished me.

She handed me a pamphlet and said, "If you want to make a complaint, here's the phone number to call".

I was utterly gob smacked and left the bank.

I called the head office of the bank and made the complaint, in tears. I was told something would be done. I was also given the name and number of someone in the business-banking sector of the organization that I could ask about the proper account.

I called the number, told the person on the phone what kind of account I needed and the response was, "We set up those kinds of accounts everyday".

I was given an appointment time at yet another branch, went to the appointment and the account I needed was set up in twenty minutes without any problem. Of course due to my experiences with the other banks I needed to see if this would work. I personally tested the account at a number of branches across the city and it worked every time. I still, to this day use the account and can only attribute ignorance for the treatment I received from the other managers.

I have not had any follow up on my original complaint regarding the insensitive and rude branch manager. Tony's Promise is now a registered, non-profit corporation.

I wanted Tony's Promise to be something important. I wanted it to grow and spread the word on safe driving. I wanted it to prevent families from going through the almost unbearable pain of losing a child to such a preventable accident.

I put together a board of directors consisting of the four young men who were involved with the creation of Tony's Promise. The "fantastic four", I call them.

I wanted my daughter Alanna on the board. I also invited some of my friends with experience, as they sit on various boards of other organizations.

I was approached by Mothers Against Drunk Driving (MADD) almost daily in the first few weeks. The calls were to offer support and to invite us to the annual meeting of families who have lost loved ones to drinking and driving.

They also wanted to use a video that was created by one of the fantastic four, Parker. It is a very emotional portrayal of Tony's friends visiting the crash site with very moving music and poignant text highlighting the dangers of impaired driving. It brings most people to tears when they watch it. MADD asked me if they could incorporate Parker's video into their presentations because it was so touching.

"Will you edit anything in the video", I asked?

"Yes, we will strip out all reference to your son".

"I'm afraid I can't give you permission to use the video, besides, we still don't know if Campbell was drunk or not. How would that look if you had this great, emotional video as part of your presentation and it turned out that he was not drunk? Not good, I imagine".

I never heard from them again.

So the campaign was underway. One day a young man
named Patrick claiming to be one of Tony's friends
approached me and said, "I'm selling 'R.I.P. Tony' bumper
stickers for ten bucks each and I have almost six hundred
dollars. I'll give you the money when I get closer to a
thousand, OK"?
I had never met the young man but Alanna assured me that
he was indeed a friend, so I could only say, "great, thank you".
Sure enough, about a month later I ran into him again and he
hands me an envelope with over eight hundred dollars in it.
At the same time he said, "Look at this".
He opened his shirt and tattooed across his chest in gothic
style font is,

Anthony McColl
March 11, 1992 – April 16, 2011

"Please tell me that's temporary tattoo".
"No way, it's real".
I wanted to ask him if his parents had anything to say about
that, but decided not to. What a humbling gesture. I had
never met this kid but here he was, getting my son's name
inked on his chest and raising money for the campaign.

I thanked him, gave him a hug and made my way to the bank.
Suddenly people were contacting me asking, "Where can I get
a Tony's Promise bracelet"?

"I didn't know you could"?

"Oh yes, Carole has had some made up, they're three dollars",
said my daughter.

Carole and her boyfriend Dan were good friends of Tony's
and I ran into her at a gas station a few weeks later. Once
again, I was handed a wad of cash from the sale of Tony's
Promise bracelets. I was speechless.

We had to get some formality around this thing. I contacted a
friend in the promotional marketing business and had
bracelets designed and ordered 250 of them. I decided to
maintain the white theme as the students at D'Arcy McGee
High School had done, the Monday following the accident.
Black on white, coincidence maybe, but when Anthony was
first born, Monica and I decided that his room should have
maximum contrast in terms of color scheme, black and white.
So it seemed fitting to keep the Tony's Promise theme black
and white.

During one of our first board meetings Richard said, "We need something that will be a constant reminder to teens when they are driving. We need a key chain that says "I Promise" so every time they get in the car and start it, they see that key chain and they will know that they must drive carefully".

Brilliant idea.

I called my friend Katie who is a graphic designer. I asked if she wouldn't mind designing a touching logo that kids would like and said 'I Promise' and 'Tony's Promise' on it.

Hence, the heart hands were created.

Then Parker kicked in and said "let's get hats, teenagers love hats". He designed a different hat logo and we got hats as well.

I had no idea how the campaign would grow, but schools had music concerts to create awareness and raise money.

In the spring, we give Tony's Promise presentations for "Safe Prom" at high schools and in hospitals in conjunction with Prevent Alcohol and Risk Related Trauma in Youth (P.A.R.T.Y.)

Members of the Tony's Promise Facebook group regularly send me stories of how they kept the "Promise". Here are a few.

Submitted by H.O. on September 4, 2011

"I thought I'd let you know I called the police on a drunk 18 year old kid last night. My friend and I were in town picking up her boyfriend from one of the bars at the end of the night when we watched this kid stumble up and down the curb from the top of the street to the bottom. We were laughing initially because he was too drunk and just all over the place. When we drove up that street after we saw him trying to get into a car. My heart immediately stopped and I asked her to pull over. I got out of the car and asked him if he was okay and he responded NO I cant get my car open. (I found out that it wasn't his car let alone the right make of car). I told him that I had watched him stumble up the street when he told me he was just getting his ID so he could go back to the bars. Keep in mind

this was the end of the night, almost two o'clock and just now he was getting his ID? I wasn't falling for it and I was not going to leave him alone. He kept on trying one car after another thinking it was his car. He then asked me where are we, in Montreal? I said we're in Hull (two hours east of Montreal) and he just looked even more confused. I knew at that point that something had to be done. My friend's boyfriend stayed talking to him while I went back to the car and called 911. I told the kid I had lost a friend because of a drunk driver and was not about to let him anywhere near his car. Within minutes the police arrived and he was taken care of. It terrifies me to think that a guy, who thought he was in Montreal was planning on driving home to Brockville, which is one hour away from Hull."

Submitted by J. G., October, 2011 about his daughters.
"I've been a member of the Tony's Promise group for a while and I know that the message will get through.

I wrote that as a proud parent knowing that the message is getting through to my Kids and their friends.

I woke up early on Sunday morning and noticed than our vehicle wasn't there, then I noticed the note that explained the situation.

My 2 daughters decided to take a taxi home from a party the previous night. To my surprise when we drove back to pick up the van, I noticed a few more cars were left behind from the previous night.

It was a proud moment and I wrote my daughters a note as my way of letting them know how I felt.

This is what I wrote on the note;

There's not a better feeling in the world than to see a note saying that the Van isn't there because my daughters took a taxi home from a party".

A Concerned Mother, December, 2011

"Hello David,

My son who is now at Heritage and was a D'Arcy McGee High School student also knew your son Anthony. As a matter of fact, he was at the same party the night of the accident. I had instructed him to NOT accept a ride from anyone in order to get back home but instead to stay at the house where the party was OR to phone me - no matter what time - and I would get him. I got a call from him in the middle of the night saying that someone could drive him back and I said NO. I then got a call from him the next morning around 11 am and all he said was "mom, a boy got killed". I don't think I ever felt so sick or numb.

He told me what happened and I cried all day, and I cried all week even though I did not know your son. I have cried every time since when there is a report of another teenage driver who has been killed in a car accident.

My son has always been a very responsible person and he has since embraced Tony's Promise. He has never taken off the bracelet and spreads the message to everyone who is willing to listen. I am very proud of him and all his friends and the actions they take to keep everyone safe. I think the initiative is wonderful and will save a lot of lives.

This is why I am writing to you. I would like to give you an example. My son went to a party last week with some of his closest friends. They were supposed to be picked up by a mother of one of the friends when an incident at the party caused them to go looking for someone who had left the party. They all spread out and searched the neighbourhood. My son and two friends were in a park when they heard a loud sound. They said it sounded like a car had hit something. They were at a major intersection but obviously late at night with not much traffic or other help. They sprinted to the street to see an SUV with a lone driver trying to get off a curb but repeatedly hitting the curb violently, causing the car tires to go flat and causing great damage to the car. They decided that they had to stop *this person from continuing on their journey and jumped into action. The two other boys went up to the car, knocked on the window and saw the driver "zoned out" as they described it and started talking to him - trying to get him to surrender his keys and get out of the car. The driver was determined to get back to Ottawa. In the meantime my son was on the phone with the police, describing everything and telling them because of "Tony's Promise" they can't let this guy go anywhere. They eventually talked him out of the car, he gave up his keys to the boys and they kept him sitting on the curb until police showed up. They were commended for their actions by the police officer and felt pretty good about themselves and the fact that their actions stopped this man from trying to drive to Ottawa and possibly killing himself or someone else. He was about 35 years old, lived in Ottawa and had been drinking at a local bar in Aylmer.*

I was very proud of all of them. I would hope that the word spreads and they can serve as an example to bring some change.

I am still in awe as to how you are coping and how you use your energy for all these great projects in Tony's honour. I respect you for all the courage and strength you continue to have. I know that I could not deal with it in such a graceful manner. But know that you are changing things! "

Haillie in Edmonton, June 2012

"Hello David,

I started working at McDonald's here in Edmonton - and I do get quite a few young drivers come through drinking & they think it's funny - and I tell them it's not funny it's not a joke, your endangering yourself and everyone around you. They all drive off of course because it's only a drive thru, but there's at least 8 cars I've written down the license plates and I've called the cops - the cops work with my McDonald's ..it's a check stop area and I would never want to wake up another morning having to hear some innocent person's life has been taken away. Tony's Promise has opened so many people's eyes and this is an amazing organization! Everyone has a right to live their full life, it shouldn't be cut short because of some irresponsible people in this world. So yes, I do respect Tony's Promise and I try my best to report the impaired drivers. <3"

I think we are saving at least a few lives.

Tony's Travelling Ashes

My wife and I had the expected discussion regarding interring my son's cremated remains. We decided that we would bury his ashes in our local cemetery with his maternal grandparents. About a month after the accident, my daughter said that she had heard something regarding his ashes that was mentioned by a close friend, Sam. It was something about a discussion Anthony and Sam had a few months prior to the crash. The conversation revolved around what they wanted to happen to them in the event of their death. Even though young people discuss death and mortality at least once in their lives, it was an ominous thought that the conversation took place.

I contacted Sam and asked if this discussion actually did happen. Apparently, my son said that when he died, he wanted "to be cremated and have his ashes spread all over the place".

"Ya, that's pretty much what he said", Sam replied.

So, what do we do about that, I asked my wife?

My sister was, as expected, very supportive following the accident and she spent a lot of time at my house. Upon hearing about the discussion Anthony and Sam had, she recalled that my family travelled to Vancouver Island in British Columbia two years prior and visited Long Beach near Tofino. Tofino is a beautiful town on the west coast of the island on the Pacific Ocean. It is a haven for surfing and whale watching. Both Alanna and Anthony had a wonderful time swimming in the Pacific and on our whale-watching trip in a twenty-foot hard-hulled inflatable boat. Anthony later announced that Long Beach was the most beautiful place he had ever visited.

Knowing this, my sister quickly jumped in and said "I'm going to Long Beach in a few weeks, would you like me to take some of his ashes with me and spread them on the beach"? We thought that would be a great idea and agreed.

Knowing that my sister is a very detailed researcher, a few days before her trip she contacted me and said, "OK, I have checked with the airlines and in order for me to transport Anthony's ashes, I'll need a copy of his death certificate and the cremation certificate".

"No problem, but take photos when you spread the ashes, maybe I'll post them on Tony's Promise Face Book group so that everybody understands what you are doing", I said.

After gathering the necessary documents, I poured about a teaspoon of ashes in a pill bottle and placed everything in a large freezer bag. Thus creating what would come to be known as an "ashes kit".

I shared this great idea with my friends Rick and Peggy Henderson and they thought it was a beautiful thing to do. A few days later Rick called me and said, "We are going to Egypt in a few weeks and, if it's OK with you, we would like to take some of Anthony's ashes to spread somewhere over there".

"Come on guys, you don't have to interrupt your holiday by going out of your way to spread his ashes, it's your vacation".

"No", no said Rick.
"We would be honored to do this and I'll take a lot of pictures".
"Could you spread them in the dessert with the Pyramids in the background"?
"Of course, let me look after it, but only if you don't mind"
"We would be delighted if you did that for us"

And so started "Tony's Traveling Ashes".

My sister traveled to Tofino and called me a few days later, very excited.

"Dave, you have to see the photo of me spreading the ashes. I mixed them with some beach sand and threw them up in the air while Murray took a few photos. The ashes have taken the shape of a large man running toward the ocean. It looks like Anthony".

She emailed me the photograph and sure enough, the ashes have taken the form of a person making their way to the water. Many other people see this in the photo as well.

Needless to say we decided not to bury Anthony's ashes for a while as many requests came in from friends and family to have the honor of spreading a part of my son in various parts of the world. As of the writing of this book, with the help of many friends and family, Tony's Ashes have been scattered in the following countries;

Egypt

Tanzania

Brazil

Peru

England

Numerous locations in Canada

Vietnam

Japan

Italy

The Vatican

South Africa

Israel

New Zealand

Australia

Germany

The following are photographs of some of the places where Tony's ashes have been scattered to date. Each location listed is accompanied by the writing of the people scattering the ashes and it includes the emotion they felt while doing so. Most were brought to tears as am I while reading their heart-felt commentary. I am deeply humbled that my friends and family have offered to do this. Thank you all so much.

Long Beach, Tofino, British Columbia

This is the first spreading of Tony's ashes at one of his favorite places, Long Beach on Vancouver Island, British Columbia. We vacationed there in 2007 and had a great time. He loved the water and the temperate climate. Tony and Alanna swam in the Pacific Ocean (the only 2 people not wearing wet suits to stay warm in the icy water). Monica and I watched sitting on the beach, watching whales breaching in the distance. It was a truly magical vacation. The ashes were tossed into the air **by Tony's Auntie "Jo-dan"**, David's sister. Notice how the **flying ashes** have taken the shape of a large person running **toward the** water. (This photo was not edited in any way)

The Pyramids, Egypt

Hi Dave and Monica, we wanted to drop you a note about our travels and especially about the very special moments we had with Anthony in Egypt. We really felt like he was accompanying us through all of our travels to some very special places but we were very aware of his presence in the two places where we left his ashes.

Egypt was everything we wanted it to be and more. The sites are overwhelming in their size, their age, their magnificence and their history. We will always remember the sights and sounds of Cairo and Luxor – some good, some not so good - but most of all the memories of our moments with Anthony will always be indelibly etched in our hearts and memory.

At Giza we toured around the Great Pyramids and the Sphinx

in 38-degree heat, and took in their awesome presence for a

few hours. Then, Peggy and I got on two camels and were led

into the desert by two young Bedouin boys, while we slowly

rode to a lonely place with no one else around us. I decided

that this was to be the perfect spot for Anthony at Giza. I

snapped a picture of Peggy and Anthony's ashes with the

Pyramids in the background. It was quiet. There was a cooling

breeze and the sun was blazing hot. We rode back quietly.

From the spot where Anthony's ashes lay, you can see all of the

eleven Pyramids of Giza.

Two days later, we arrived at Dashur's high desert plateau,

where the Bent Pyramid and the Great Red Pyramid of

Pharaoh Snefru are located. The Red Pyramid is the third

largest in Egypt. Again, the heat was intense and the breeze

quite strong.

We walked around the Pyramids then climbed the scary steps

up to the entrance tunnel of the Red Pyramid so high above the

desert. Peggy descended about thirty meters but then had to

turn back, being somewhat claustrophobic; the tunnel is three

feet wide by four feet high. So, I continued down until I

reached the bottom, and slowly walked through the first and

second chambers. The chambers are magnificent, with high,

corbelled ceilings. It's hot and the air is close. There is a large wooden staircase in the second chamber that leads to the third and final chamber. This is the burial chamber of Snefru; ancient Egyptians called it the resurrection chamber.

There was only silence. I took the vial from my pocket and opened it. I paused to take in the awesome and magnificent place where I found myself and then I poured Anthony's ashes into the burial chamber, making the sign of the cross. Because of where I was I smiled and said; "Assalamu alaikum, Anthony. I hope you will share the heavens with Jesus, Mohammed, Osiris and Isis".

When I went back up the entrance tunnel where Peggy had spent forty minutes with the Pyramids caretaker, Peggy said to me as she stood there looking out over the desert, what she saw was Anthony's face shining everywhere in the desert, wherever she looked, then she sang "Amazing Grace". At this we both cried an left. Love always, Rick and Peggy.

Stonehenge

We were meeting our daughter Chrystelle, in London, UK and we had the privilege of being part of 'Tony's Travelling Ashes'.

Although before leaving we had an idea of the perfect location for Anthony, we left with an open mind. Everywhere we went, Tony was with us...

At The Globe Theater, a reproduction of Shakespeare's first theater we thought it could be a tribute to Anthony's interest in the arts, but we dismissed it, it is a mere replica after all. The Polo match we attended could have been a tribute to Tony's athleticism, but I had an issue with the horses possibly trampling over him (once a mother always a mother). The Ye Olde Cheshire Cheese Pub, the oldest pub in London, which was rebuilt after the great fire in 1668 where Mark Twain, Sir Arthur Conan Doyle and Charles Dickens enjoyed a few brews, was a possibility. The pub evoked Tony's endurance and determination, his love of the arts and of a good time. The Cheshire Cheese Pub was getting closer to the appropriate spot! Then there was the magical moment we experienced at Westminster Abby, listening to the choir while sitting in the royal choir stalls. Befitting of Royalty... a possibility.

But, as we approached Stonehenge, our original idea, we thought 'this may be it'. We took an early, very early morning tour that allowed us to walk among the boulders. The majesty of Stonehenge was fitting! Its unexplained history echoed the miracle of Tony's being, its timelessness mirrored the impact of Tony's life, the boulders evoked Tony's strength, yet the soft green grass reminded us of his kindness. With the warmth of the sun on our faces, we released Tony's ashes.

Thank you for allowing us to be part of this commemoration of who Tony is.

Jo-Anne, Claude and Chrystelle.

Pine Lodge, Bristol, Quebec

The Shawville Fair falls on Labour Day weekend every year and since my birthday does as well, I've always gone with numerous friends over the years. For the last four years Tony has been part of that. We'd usually stay the weekend at Pine Lodge, a small campground about fifteen minutes before Shawville with my grandparents. Of course, the weekend would consist of some really good memories, a few beers and bonfires on the beach and a LOT of laughs.

Tony loved the weekend that he got to get away for a few days with some good friends and that's why we found it overly appropriate to send some of his ashes away in the water that weekend, on a beach that meant a lot to him. For all the people that made this weekend as special as it was for Tony,

this was done with you in mind.

Jessa Leduc

Mount Kilimanjaro, Tanzania, Africa

Hi Dave, Monica and Alanna. I set out in January to climb to the rooftop of Africa, Mount Kilimanjaro. It stands 19, 341 feet above sea level and is still an active volcano. Each day was a new adventure form sleeping in the rainforest and being awakened by the calabus monkeys to climbing the 800-foot cliff of the Barancco Wall. I couldn't wait to see what each day had in store. Finally, after seven days of trekking through 4 vegetation zones and testing our bodies at various altitudes we were ready to make the final ascent to Uhuru Peak. On February 2 after eight hours and forty minutes of steep uphill, switchback trail which begins over rock, but quickly turns to volcanic scree – resembling loose gravel, we arrived! There it was, the sign indicating we had reached the summit of the tallest freestanding mountain in the world! There were tears

and hugs of congratulations.

During my trek I met some wonderful people and was able to share Tony's story as well as tell them about a family I admire. Your strength to carry out Tony's wishes and to share his story in an effort to raise awareness and save lives is one of the most selfless acts I can imagine. I want you to know that Tony was with me every step of the way. I am happy to share my success and feel privileged to have shared in such an intimate undertaking. Before releasing the ashes, my guides informed me that Uhuru is Swahili for freedom. I felt quite moved knowing that a little piece of Tony would remain here, free, at the summit forever! This moment will forever be embedded in my memory.

Thank you for allowing me to be part of Tony's Traveling Ashes.
Nicole R.

Mount Fuji, Japan

Having followed the weather every day, looking for a break in the uniformly grim forecasts, Helen and I did the trek to Mt. Fuji on Saturday, starting off on the Shinkansen Kodama at Maibara, not far from where she lives in Hikone. We rented a car near the train station at Shinfuji, and ran smack into half the population of Honshu going north to experience Zen Views of Fuji-San from The Five Lakes District during Golden Week. Apparently this can only be done using your SUV. Traffic, however, cleared up instantly on the road to Fujinomiya Fifth Station, about two-thirds up the mountain.

Excessive snow had caused considerable damage to the station, but things were still functioning. The snow also meant that we would have had to have technical equipment to go up much further. We found a small, secluded spot off the trail, just below the tree line, and scattered Anthony's ashes. The brief cloud of ash disappeared almost instantly in the air against the snow, and we reflected that Fuji-San will look after him well.

Helen took a moment to re-create a small Shinto ceremony involving some coins and a prayer for peace. It was a beautiful, beautiful day.

Our profound thanks to you all, for giving us the honor of remembering our friend in this way.

Love, John, Helen and Lynn.

Key Largo, Florida

Key Largo is best known for its fabulous restaurants, beautiful beaches and gorgeous sunsets. Sailboats moor along pristine shores lined with mangrove. I was honored to be able to scatter some of Anthony's ashes in the ocean in Key Largo's Everglades National Park.

I was Anthony's grade six teacher, and as a teacher, every student is precious to me. I hope that you will all take Tony's Promise seriously. When you have been out having fun please stop a moment and think about Anthony. Drinking and driving, or getting into a car with a drunk driver is always a bad idea.

Take care of yourself and your friends. Barbara Holland.

The Maritimes, Eastern Canada

This photo was taken by Michael Carty, a talented photographer from Digby Nova Scotia. It is a shot of a good family friend scattering Tony's ashes into the Atlantic Ocean. Tony loved to watch the sunrise and he loved water. He also loved wearing a hoodie, as some of you know. This shot was taken at sunset. You can see Michael Carty's portfolio at the following link;

http://michaelcartyphotography.com

Keep the promise and stay safe.

Vietnam

We took this picture on Anthony's birthday, March 11th, at the Po Nagar Temple on the banks of the Cai River in Nha Trang, Vietnam. The Vietnamese believe that death destroys only the physical body, for the souls survive in the hereafter and have the capacity to intervene in the lives of the living. The deceased thus maintains relations with his or her family. Each individual invokes his ancestors at the alter, thus demonstrating his veneration and expressing his wishes. Anthony will be with us forever.

Love,
Auntie Jodan and Murray

The Coliseum, Rome

Anthony had both the physical appearance and brave spirit
that symbolized the ancient Roman gladiators. We tossed
Anthony's ashes into the crisp Italian air with the stunning
backdrop of the Roman Coliseum framing the photo because
we thought he could have been one of them.

Love,
Auntie Jodan and Murray

Santa Anna Riverbed, Riverside, California

Wow, this will be great, what an honor, my husband and I said to one another. We were taking Anthony McColl's ashes with us on our trip to Southern California. The excitement was however, a bit short-lived as reality hit: holy cow... where were we going to spread his ashes in a place that will be both

sentimental and meaningful? I became panicked, looking to my husband for support, but stopped myself short as I noticed the same expression on his face. 'What's the matter, I asked? He, it turns out was having his own holy cow moment about being the official photographer and getting the perfect picture to bring home to the McColl's.

As luck would have it, I raised this challenge with some former students. One said, quite brilliantly, Ms., why don't you spread his ashes in the forest? He had just finished his Forest Fire Fighter course". As I said, a brilliant idea... until it dawned on me, the last time that I checked, Southern California wasn't brimming with forests as much as it was full of deserts.

After much deliberation, this is what my husband and I came up with. My aunt and uncle live in Riverside, CA just above the old Santa Ana river bottom. Located where it is, it's been dry for quite some time. Actually, because that whole area of Southern California is dry, it's not uncommon for brush to light on fire, causing varying levels of damage. My aunt and uncle were aware of this when they purchased their home, so they planted 'ice plant' in their back yard between their property line and the top of the river bottom. The concept of ice plant is similar to aloe vera, but instead of the leaves being home to aloe, they are the home to water. The idea is that if the river *bottom catches on fire (which has happened) and the fire spreads up the bank, when it gets to the ice plant, the fire breaks the leaves, which releases the water which saves the home and the people inside it (which, thank fully has also happened). We thought this would be perfect, given Tony's desire to be a Forest Fire Fighter, something he was supposed to do this past summer. So now, even though Tony's body won't be able to fight the fires, his ashes and spirit will help keep people and their homes safe.*

Erin M. and her husband Gavin.

Christ The Redeemer, Rio De Janerio, Brazil

Dear friends,

Jean-Louis and I have returned from Brazil, including Rio de Janeiro, where we had the honor of spreading Tony's ashes. We were travelling with our friends from France and were also accompanied by a Carioca, Paulo, who showed us the sights of Rio.

When we explained Tony's story and our desire to spread his ashes, Paulo suggested Corcovado (Christ The Redeemer), not so much for its religious significance (although there are those who take solace from that), but because of the sites beauty and because of its commanding view of Rio and Sugarloaf.

We therefore enlisted the help of our international entourage to take some photos as we went up the mountain and finally as we reached the summit. Everyone in our group was deeply affected by the ceremony and the meaning of Tony's Promise.

Even if we don't live forever, our actions and legacies have a chance of doing so. To Dave, Monica and Alanna, I wish to express my enormous respect for your grace as you live through this. To Tony, your legacy is already affecting many and more... you live on.

Sincerely yours, George P.

Our first ash spreading ceremony was on the Great Wall of China. The view was spectacular. It was quiet a challenge to get the wind to cooperate with us but we finally managed.

Our second ash spreading ceremony was at Base Camp, Mount Everest. We had a bigger challenge there – The Red Army. Our Tibetan guide insisted we ask permission first. After 15 - 20 minutes of debate between our guide and the Chinese soldiers, our request was denied. Leaving the checkpoint (may I say, "pissed off") we ventured closer to the Base Camp and further away from the checkpoint, we decided "the hell with this" and released Tony's ashes.

We consider ourselves very privileged to have had Anthony with us during this memorable trip.

Sincerely, Nancy Jane and Pierre

Lake Bernard, Quebec

Friends and family spread his ashes at the cottage on Lake Bernard. Some say that the ashes look like a dove taking flight.

Firsts

There have been entire books written on how to deal with the series of "firsts" following the death of a family member, particularly the loss of a child.

The accident occurred on April 16, 2011. People didn't start asking about what we were going to do for Christmas until October. What a thought, Christmas without my son. He loved Christmas. He probably enjoyed Christmas so much because we almost always got both of our children exactly what they asked for. Other than that Christmas was pretty much what you would call normal, midnight mass on Christmas Eve, up the next morning to too many presents and too much food. The usual Christmas day dinner at the home of relatives. But we were together and we had fun. When he was young, we would get Anthony Lego for Christmas. He adored Lego and from the moment he opened his gifts he would sit and put his Lego blocks together and wouldn't stop until whatever he was building was completed.

First Christmas

What would we do this Christmas? We discussed it together and considered a few options. Should we just push on ahead and do what we normally do? Should we change our routine in some significant way? Should we go away somewhere? Whatever we do is going to be very sad and difficult.

About two weeks before December 25, Alanna announced that she had some friends coming over to work on a group project for school. There would be Jordan, Meagan, Vanessa and Hodan. No problem, they're all great kids that we know well and whose company we enjoy.

A few days later the "project team" came to the house. In walks Hodan, an intelligent and gifted athlete originally from Somalia. She walks in the house and says "Hi, where's your Christmas tree"?

"Oh, we haven't put it up yet".

"Oh, that's too bad because, being a Muslim I have never seen a Christmas tree before"

Suddenly a light went on in my head.

"If you want to come back next week and if it's OK with your parents, you can help us decorate it".

"Really, I'd love to do that" She said with a big smile.

"Well, I'm picking it up on Monday, so how about you come by on Monday evening and we can decorate your first Christmas tree. But make sure your parents are OK with it, I don't want you to get in any trouble".

"I would love that", she replied.

So the following Monday, Hodan, Alanna and few other friends completely decorated our tree in two hours.

That helped a lot to see a young Muslim girl very happily decorate her first Christmas tree. What a perfect thing to do. It was different but not too different for us.

Christmas day was a very sad day for me.

We woke up at the normal time, went downstairs, put on the coffee and sat by the tree surrounded by fewer than normal presents.

It just didn't feel right and there was no way it was going to. It was quieter than past Christmases and I could almost feel the sad discomfort that Monica and Alanna were feeling. Not a peep of complaint from either of them.

Anthony's physical presence was greatly missed, as you would imagine. We could do nothing about it except get through it.

First Father's Day

Of course, the weeks and days leading up to the first father's day since the crash, I started to feel it again. The dull aching in my chest slowly building. I knew why. I didn't need to figure out why my sadness was once again slowly billowing in my heart. What would I do? How would I handle this event? In the years when my son was alive we would play golf on Father's Day. One year, when Anthony was employed at The Royal Ottawa Golf and Country Club he was very proud to take me for a quick round on "The Royal Nine". On one particular Father's Day we made it through three holes and the sky began to darken. Large cumulus clouds slowly rolled into the area. The sudden cold wind associated with the down drafts of the storm began, pulling cold air from many thousands of feet above. Then the rain started. Heavy, torrential rain. We were lucky as the car was not far off and we managed to jump in before getting too wet. We sat there and watched as the rain and hail came down in what I can only describe as "biblical proportions". And we were together. A father and his son sitting in the car, dampened by a June thunderstorm that interrupted our golf game. But it didn't matter. We were doing something we loved to do and we were together.

What would I do this year? On that first Father's Day after I lost my favorite golfing partner, I got into my car and drove out of my driveway. It was a beautiful, sunny day and I thought, 'why not go down to the local marina and have a look around'? There would be lot of activity and it would be a good distraction. I was right, it was very busy. I parked the car and walked along the paved path with the throngs of families and cyclists passing by. I headed to the boat launch area. This is where people launch and recover their boats, often two at a time, side by side. I don't think I could have chosen a more interesting thing to do. Cars and trailers were lined up to get to the launch. Cars would inch their way down the ramp, easing the trailer as far into the water as safely as possible. Often the spouse would be directing the driver down the ramp and, once stopped in the water, undo the various straps that fastened the boat to the trailer. The boat would be released and the vehicle and trailer driven away and parked. Off they would go for a day of fishing or just darting around the river.

Sometimes things wouldn't go so well. Trailers would jack-knife slightly. Husbands would curse at their helpers. Often a spouse or one of their offspring. Boaters, anxious to get on the water and get fishing would try to speed up the process and accidentally slip off of the trailer into the river, bringing on more cursing. When removing the boat from the water, straps would sometimes be forgotten and the car would drive up the ramp, leaving the unsecured boat in the water, with a bewildered helper wondering how they could forget to tie the boat to the trailer.

It was very entertaining and I have often visited the marina on sunny Sunday afternoons for a chuckle. The sadness in my heart abated for a little while. I thought of my Anthony during that time but the pain was reduced by this humorous distraction. Another opportunity to smile again. I think I'll make this a regular Father's Day ritual.

First Birthday

When my son died on April 16, he had only been 19 years old for a month. His birth date was March 11, 1992. I will always be saddened by the fact that he never made it beyond his teenaged years. Every March 11th will be sad for me but the first March 11th that followed the crash was obviously filled with anxious, gut wrenching foreboding. It felt similar to the lead up to Christmas but my internal feeling of sadness was much more intense. It felt as if I would start crying at any moment without any control over it and no matter where I was. Oddly, I didn't feel the usual anvil in my chest growing this time. Perhaps that was a sign of being better able to handle my grief. This of course, creates two internal feelings. The first is one of relief. The fact that I will survive, maybe I am starting to be able to deal properly with the grief process. The second is the feeling of guilt. A little nagging feeling deep in my mind, the small devil in my head that says, "Ha, you heartless bastard, you're forgetting your son"! This guilt of course, conjures up more feelings of sadness.

Once again, Monica, Alanna and I discussed what we should do. One thought was to simply try to have a normal day, but that would be difficult. Anthony's 20th birthday, the first birthday since the crash was on a Sunday, March 11. Sunday is our mandatory "everyone home for dinner" day. We usually eat together every day but Sunday is sacrosanct, dinner together is not optional. The thought of it still brings tears to my eyes.

What to do? We thought of staying home and avoiding all contact with the outside world but that was an unhealthy choice. Because we are people that love life we decided very soon after the accident that we were not going to let our grief get the better of us.

Perhaps we would have some of his close friends over for dinner but he had so many close friends there was no way our small house could comfortably accommodate them all.

The week prior to March 11, I ran into a friend mine.

His son and Anthony had been friends since they were in grade school. During our chat my friend asked, "What are you doing for Anthony's birthday"?

"We're not sure yet".

"Anita and I were thinking of dropping by with a birthday cake".

"Please don't do that", was all I could say.

How macabre and uncomfortable would that be?

He is gone, so why pretend he isn't. Again, this was a gesture intended to make us feel better, offered by a friend who only wants to help and can't imagine what we are going through.

It is difficult for people to know what to do when they want to help you so much.

Monica brought up the idea of asking some of his close friends out for dinner at Anthony's favorite birthday restaurant?

It would definitely not be a birthday celebration, but a gathering of his friends on his birthday, to chat and see how they were doing. That was what we would do. I called the restaurant to make a reservation but it had closed the previous year. What to do? Well, he worked in a local restaurant, why not go there?

And so we did. I spoke to Anthony's former boss and about 15 of us got together on

Sunday, March 11 and had dinner. No tears, no discussion about him dying, just us having dinner with a bunch of his close friends.

Justin, one of Anthony's very close friends had offered to pick us up and drive us to the restaurant. After dinner, we were in Justin's car on the way home and we could hear very comforting, soft music that was playing on his iPhone that was plugged into the car's sound system.

It was music that you would hear in a spa. I looked at the iPhone and realized that it was Anthony's phone. After retrieving it from the car, Monica and I agreed to give it to Justin, as I knew he was in the market for a new cell phone.

Before I gave it to him, I had to have it "unlocked". This is done so that any service provider can connect to the phone and it is not rendered useless. In order to unlock the phone, the memory first must be completely erased. Doing so essentially erases everything from the internal memory, emails, text messages, photos, video, etc.

"Is that Anthony's phone", I asked?

"Yep, that's his, and this is his music. Oddly enough, wherever you had the phone unlocked they managed to save everything on it. I have all of his music, his messages, his video, everything. This song is "Padmasana" by Buckethead. Anthony loved this music. He used to listen to this song when he was cruising in the car."

Well, that was it, the combination of the lovely, flowing guitar melody and the fact that somehow all of my son's music was saved on his phone was too much. Monica started crying and so did I. We pulled into the driveway, thanked Justin and went into the house in sobs. Tears that were a long time in coming because we didn't cry during dinner, but they came and they felt good.

The Burial and First Anniversary of the Accident

On the eve of the first anniversary of the crash, I wrote my thoughts in a Face Book message on the Tony's Promise group. It was one year to the second and recounted the last conversation I had with my son.

"It is April 15, 2012 at 2:00PM. Exactly one year ago at this second, I sat in the very chair I am now occupying. You were sitting across the table from me. We had both finished work and school and arrived home early. You had just started watching the movie "District 9" and you welcomed me to watch it with you. During the movie we chatted about the up-coming forest fire season and how we both hoped that you would get hired somewhere in Ontario. I remember telling you how proud I was for all of the hard work and time you put into the training, without a single complaint. I thought about the tremendous pride I had in you for making the decision to become a Fire Ranger. A difficult and very dangerous job.

In the 4 weeks prior to your death we epitomized the word "bonding". We worked together to prepare you for the upcoming fitness test as well as the week of classroom training. Those days could not have been more enjoyable for me and I wish every father could have the same experience with his son.

It was 3:45 when the movie finished, and you walked across the kitchen toward the door.

"I'm going to work", you said.

"Drive carefully", was my usual response, knowing full well that you always drove carefully. You walked out the door, passed by the window to the car. I was happy and so very proud.

17 hours later I saw you again, in the worst circumstances a parent can imagine. That site will be etched in my memory forever. But when I relive that scene in my head, it gets pushed away by all of the great moments we had as a father and son and as a family.

You were taken far too early and I will cherish our last days together."

I knew that I would feel sad in the days and weeks leading up to the first anniversary. I didn't know how bad I would feel. Four days prior to the burial I felt the most profound sadness I had experienced since my son's death. I didn't remember ever feeling that sad since then. I attribute that to being beyond the feelings of shock and disbelief, which are a bit of a blessing. Shock is helpful in that it provides a buffer to the pain of grief. Almost a year later I'm well beyond accepting that my son is never coming back. I'm learning to live with my "new normal" and there are parts of the day where I am distracted enough to not think about him. I'm not even worrying too much about the guilt that comes from not thinking about my son. But when the sadness starts to build there is no shock related buffer or protection from the sadness after so many months. It's almost unbearable. Everything is a chore and difficult to think about. I need to cut the grass. I'll have to get out the lawn mower, put gas in it and traipse around with that smelly, noisy thing and I just can't do that.

It's very difficult. On that same day, I run into my friend David Perry. Just speaking to people is a like running a marathon. I don't want to talk, I just want to walk past and go to the bathroom and be alone. But I don't. I talk to David because he is my friend. He too is struggling with grief. He is uncomfortable knowing the anniversary is approaching. Not knowing really what to say. What can people say? There's nothing you can say except hello, followed by small talk. And I plow through it. I don't want to be rude or mean, I just want the pain and sadness to stop. As our Psychologist says; "You just put your head down, grit your teeth and drive through the pain. You'll never get over it, just through it". I can't explain the feeling of that pain. I can only say that it went away a few days later almost as quickly as it appeared.

I had a strong urge to contact Brian Campbell's family and offer them some sort of comfort and let them know that we were thinking of them on the anniversary but Monica suggested against that. She thought it would be too painful for them. I took her advice and didn't call.

About eight months after the crash a number of Anthony's friends contacted me about where they could go to pay their respects. They wanted to know where he was buried so they could bring flowers and say a prayer. I would tell them that since Tony's Traveling Ashes we had decided to wait to bury him. We did so because we wanted to keep ashes for his travels around the globe. Monica and I decided that it was time for a traditional burial. His friends deserved that. So we decided that we would have a full burial ceremony on the first anniversary of the crash, April 16. But April 16, 2012 was a Monday and that would mean that fewer people would be able to attend. So the decision was made to bury our son on Saturday, April 14, so as many people as possible could attend. We would follow the burial with a light lunch at the church where we had the funeral. Two hundred and fifty people showed up. It was wonderful.

I decided to build an urn to bury him in. It would be plain pine with no finish on it, as I wanted it to be completely biodegradable. The idea of pine also came to mind because his goal was to become a forest fire fighter. Had he lived long enough to become a "Fire Ranger", he would have battled burning pine trees all summer. So that seemed fitting.

We had the usual ceremony with a touching speech by Father Bill, our Parish Priest. We went back to the church, had a bite to eat and I decided to give a short speech. The speech was an opportunity to have a lot of the people that supported us together in the same room at the same time. I wanted to let them all know how their support is helping to get us through this horrible time. It was the most difficult speech I have ever delivered. I couldn't get through five words without choking up. I was pacing and there were long pauses between words. It was very discomforting. I wanted to thank these people so badly and I was screwing it up. During one of these long breaks, a good friend of mine. David Perry, a writer and highly experienced public speaker shouted out.

"Give us an update on Tony's Travelling Ashes"

That snapped me back into it. I gave an update. Then he said,

"Tell them about your book". Another cue that helped.

A few days later he apologized for doing that but I said.

"Hey, no need to apologize, I knew exactly why you did it and I appreciate it so much. I was getting way off track and too emotional to speak so you kept bringing me back. It was perfect. Thank you for that".

During the post funeral get together, I invited anyone to come up on stage to offer any memories they had of my son and few got up and shared some memorable stories. David Perry's son Corey got up to speak. He had been Anthony's friend when they were very young. Corey told a funny story about getting into the house by trying to climb up to a second storey window with Anthony's help. It ended in them falling out of a tree only to discover that the door was unlocked all along. Corey also talked about the importance of not losing touch with old friends as he and Anthony did. He was saddened that they had lost contact. Corey was a good friend and is now off to become a doctor at McGill University.

Towards the end of the post-burial luncheon, Anthony's friend Loic approached me. He shook my hand and I couldn't help but notice that his hands were filthy and caked with dirt.
"Dave, I have to tell you something"
What now, I thought?
"We buried Tony"
"Pardon"?
"Me, Eric and Johnny buried Tony. The cemetery guy was really busy so we decided to bury Tony. The hole was already there and we asked the cemetery guy if we could quickly bury our friend and he said OK. So we put the urn in the ground and filled it in. We buried our friend and said a

prayer."

I wasn't registering what Loic was telling me and simply said thank you. Later I processed the notion in my mind and thought, how perfect. How classic. My son literally buried by a few of his very close friends. I cry when I picture it. I can only imagine what they felt while doing it.

The burial was a milestone for me but we still had the one-year anniversary to get through.

On Sunday, the day after the burial, Monica said, I don't think I'll go in to work on the 16th. Alanna said she wanted to stay home from school as well on the 16th. I was feeling pretty good. Anthony's friends got to bury him, and there was finally a place where they could pay their respects.

"I'm going to go to work tomorrow", I said with confidence. "I'm feeling pretty good".

When I woke up on Monday, April 16, 2012, I knew I wasn't going anywhere. I woke up during the night around 3:00 AM. That was around the time the accident happened. I was very sad and wouldn't have lasted ten minutes at work. So the power of grief got to me again. I would recommend against fighting it, just do your best to get through it. Do so without the use of drugs or alcohol. You'll be happy you did.

Conclusion

Once again, all I can do is share my experience with grief and hope that people in the same position find some way of getting through the pain.

I miss my son. I miss him terribly. I wander emotionally between the fact that he is really gone and, I'm going to wake up one day, he'll come upstairs from his bedroom in the basement. He'll nonchalantly walk into the kitchen, pour a cup of coffee and cook a couple of eggs. The nightmare will be over.

Those of you who are reading this and have not lost a child are right, you can't imagine. You can only imagine it when it happens to you and you live the experience. Think about the saddest you have ever felt in your life and multiply that sadness by many thousands. You don't want to imagine, you don't want to know what it's like.

He was a good boy, full of love, compassion and kindness. He was taken from this world far too soon. I sincerely hope I will see him again. Perhaps I will in the next life.

Rest in peace my beautiful boy.

Addendum A: Closure Points "Death Errands"

Tasks that are important and easily forgotten during the blur and fog in the early stages of grief.

- Call your auto insurance company. Don't forget to enquire about cancelling the insurance on the car involved (if it was a write-off). They may even pay for part of the funeral. They may also pay for a rental for a specified period of time.

- Depending on where you live, there may be state or provincial insurance implications, so call them. Where I live, residents pay annual automobile insurance premiums to the province. Quite a few people are not aware that in the event of an injury or death related to a car accident, citizens are entitled to financial re-imbursement; I'm talking potentially thousands of dollars. Don't be intimidated by detailed application forms with lots of pages. I had to contact my son's employer and his school to have proof of education and proof of working hours including his salary.

- Contact the hospital to collect any personal items they may have.

- Arrange the obituary with a local newspaper and make sure you mention the names of immediate family members. This will help people who know you but may not have known the deceased. I really screwed this up when my mother died through my lack of funeral knowledge. Friends found out too late and said they would have liked to attend the funeral but didn't because my name was not listed in the obituary.

- Contact the police if a crime been committed. The police may also have some personal effects. They may have questions or information that you require for the insurance company, or that may be of value to you.

- My son was a legal adult so I had to pay a Notary Public to transfer his estate to my name.

- Contact the victim's employer for outstanding money's owed to the deceased.

- Check the deceased's last will and testament, if there is one.

- Contact your lawyer to ensure what you say to the media is not going to create controversy or land you in hot water-especially if there is a police investigation or a crime has been committed.

- If you have never arranged a funeral before, get help from a friend who has. Do not get all of your advice from the funeral home only. It will probably save you a lot of money.

- Get grief counseling, whether you think you need it or not. This is a must!
- Check with your employer's insurance company to see if you are entitled to any benefits such as extra time off, additional compensation or the cost of counseling is covered.
- Get help from friends with the details regarding the visitation (wake) and the funeral arrangements with the church.
- If you don't already have a will, have one made up. I didn't and had to sit through the process with my Notary. Its not pleasant having a will done up while you mourn the loss of a loved one.

Addendum B: Depression Symptoms

I am not qualified to give any advice on dealing with grief but I have been contacted by a number of people. These people are in the same situation. They have lost a family member in a horrible accident and have seen the amazing outpouring of support that the community and people in foreign countries have shown my family. I get emails from them saying they are in the same boat but have no support.

"Please help me, what do I do"? They ask.

"All I can do is share my experience of grief with you and hopefully that will help".

My first recommendation is to seek out professional help for you and those affected.

"You need counseling no matter how you feel", I say.

Everyone needs professional help in a situation like this.

I thought that I would go through a counselor and not a Psychologist. After three sessions I thought I was doing great. Then, during a session with a Psychologist that Alanna was seeing, I realized that talking with her really helped me feel better. I'm glad I was strong enough to realize I needed additional help.

Here is a list of symptoms that you may be experiencing after the loss of a child. The more of them you are experiencing, the more urgent it is for you to get help. Call your doctor and get him or her to refer to a professional.

1. When I wake up in the morning, I feel like there is nothing to look forward to.

2. I feel sad.

3. I feel worthless

4. My future seems hopeless

5. The pleasure and joy has gone out of my life

6. I have lost interest in aspects of life that used to be important to me

7. I am agitated and keep moving around

8. I feel restless or fidgety

9. I have trouble concentrating on things

10. I have chronic pain, headaches and digestive disorders

11. I have lost interest or pleasure in hobbies and activities that I once enjoyed, including sex

12. My sleep patterns are disrupted. I have insomnia, wake early in the morning, or have been oversleeping

13. I've had constant feelings of "life isn't worth living like this," thoughts of death or suicide, or suicide attempts

14. I am showing anger and aggressive behavior, lashing out or raising my voice when I normally would not

15. I am questioning my faith and beliefs

Addendum C: Workbook with Healing Questions

This section of the book is designed to help someone dealing with grief to map out his or her feelings. It is good to write these things down because the grief process can be quite "cloudy". Memories can be evasive and change. I was reluctant at first to write anything down, but I listened to friends who write for a living and I'm glad I did. Write down any feelings on the pages provided. These thoughts and feeling can relate to the questions or they can be anything you feel that you'd like to document. Go back to it periodically to see how your thoughts and feelings are changing. And remember, get professional help. See a qualified grief counselor or a Psychologist or a Psychiatrist. It will be absolutely invaluable in getting through your grief and on the path to healing. You will never "get over" the loss of your loved one. You will be better able to deal with it and continue to live your life. And you must get on with life. It will do you and no one else in the world any good, if you take steps to shorten your life by living dangerously or taking your own life. You must continue the memory of your lost loved one by talking about them and living a full life in their name. This is essential.

Write your thoughts on the pages provided.

1. Has your appetite dropped or increased since your loss?

_____

_____

_____

_____

_____

2. Have your sleep patterns changed?

_____

_____

_____

_____

_____

3. Are you religious? Have you sought out assistance from your church?

_____

_____

_____

_____

_____

4. What good feelings have you had this week/month?

_____

_____

_____

_____

5. Are you consciously doing something to be positive?

_____

_____

_____

_____

_____

6. Have you done anything fun/enjoyable with your family or by yourself? It is OK to smile, laugh and enjoy things again (in fact it is crucial that you do this)

_____

_____

_____

_____

_____

7. Do you discuss your lost loved one daily? With family, friends or people in a similar situation?

_____

_____

_____

_____

_____

8. Because of your loss, have you taken up or created a cause related to the loss (MADD, a Cancer related charity, etc.) List it/them.

_____

_____

_____

_____

_____

9. Recall and list humorous events you remember having with the deceased.

_____

_____

_____

_____

_____

10. List qualities of your deceased loved one that had an impact on you.

_____

_____

_____

_____

_____

11. Discuss events that were important to both/all of you, include your family.

_____

_____

_____

_____

_____

12. Review the struggles you had in the relationship.

_____

_____

_____

_____

13. Identify changes (in yourself) due to the loss in your life...how did I change for the good.

_____

_____

_____

_____

_____

14. Identify how the deceased changed because "I was part of their life".

_____

_____

_____

_____

_____

15. List favorite foods, scents, events, teams, holidays of the deceased, so you never forget, and to share the history of that person with others (possibly children and/or grandchildren).

_____

_____

_____

_____

_____

16. As a result of the your loss, list what rituals you may engage in to commemorate the deceased. For example, going to the favorite restaurant of the deceased on his/her birthday or serving their favorite meal on a special holiday (Christmas, plant a tree or flowers, etc.)

_____

_____

_____

_____

_____

17. Write something to the deceased, a poem or letter, thanking them for being in your life or how you feel about them.

_____

_____

_____

_____

_____

18. Write a story about the deceased; try to include your personal feelings.

_____

_____

_____

_____

_____

19. What physical exercise are you doing to stay fit during your time of grief?

_____

_____

_____

_____

_____

20. What negative feelings have you had and what, if anything did you do to try to turn them into positive feelings?

_____

_____

_____

_____

_____

21. Has your loved one's death made you a better person or a lesser person?

_____

_____

_____

_____

_____

Other Writing

The following are pieces are written by a variety of people. The first two are articles that were published in The Ottawa Citizen and MacLean's Magazine.

"The End" is an obituary article on the last page of each edition of MacLean's Magazine.

Both media articles are reprinted with permission of MacLean's Magazine and Postmedia News.

The third piece of writing is a description of a dream. Jessa Leduc, a very close and long-time friend of Anthony's contacted us about her dream. She was kind enough to allow me to share it with you.

The fourth piece is from my friend Laurie. Laurie Wilson is one of my close friends who among other things, writes for a living. It was Laurie that pushed me over the top to start writing "A Father's Tears", and I thank her for that.

If you believe that people can communicate with spirits, then you will enjoy the following text. If you don't believe that people can communicate with spirits, then I suggest you take this with a grain of salt.

Laurie has a special gift. Both she and her five-year-old daughter Chloe can apparently connect with people that have passed. I haven't completely bought into the idea of Mediums and speaking to the dead. I don't judge anyone who claims they can. One thing is clear to me. Whether I believe in it or if I think what Laurie says is hogwash, she always has positive things to say about the messages my son sends to her. So, if it is indeed hogwash, at least its positive and that helps ease my pain. You can decide for yourself.

1. The Ottawa Citizen, Saturday April 23, 2011

'There were two families devastated, two sons lost; McColls have no thoughts of vengeance, only hopes to honor their child's life'

By: Kelly Egan

"Their firstborn, a boy, is dead, age 19, because another young man drove recklessly and killed them both on Highway 148 last Saturday, on the fresh side of midnight. Others, cut out of twisted metal, were badly hurt.

In the days that followed, they've had to look at their child's lifeless face on a hospital gurney, empty his locker, make funeral arrangements, attend a school memorial for 400, put donated lasagna in the freezer, prepare a eulogy; face the broken world.

And yet, sitting at their kitchen table, weary, wrung out, they refuse to hate.

"There were two families devastated, two sons lost," said Monica Thibault, 53, the mother of **Anthony McColl***, the 19-year-old. "Let's just remember that."*

Husband David wants to reach out to the family of the other victim, Brandon Crawford, 20, of Shawville, who was involved in a police chase a few minutes before the fatal crash, just outside Luskville. Impairment is suspected. Police continue to investigate.

"It's not easy," said McColl, 55, "but you can decide to switch off hate and anger."

Instead, they talked about Anthony, his short life and his evolving legacy.

There has been an outpouring of love for Anthony, who throughout his life was called Ant, Anto, Antman, and finally, Tony.

A group of friends has created a Facebook page, a YouTube video, a grassroots movement, that is giving shape to a foundation, possibly called Tony's Promise.

It asks young people to pledge they will not drive while impaired and do their best to prevent their friends from doing the same.

David, a consultant, photographer and community-theatre enthusiast, has been occupied this week with how to structure such a foundation -where funds should be directed, logos, programs, literature, speakers, possibly scholarships -while cloaked in grief.

Not for a second, he says, was he filled with corrosive vengeance. "It will eat you up and kill you. I'm already eaten up by the loss of my son."

Instead, they are trying to ensure Anthony's youthful spirit lives on.

He was always big for his age, eventually growing to six-foot-four, 240 pounds, the body of a rugby player, the sport he loved *best.*

He was musical, playing the drums and singing in a band called Hostility, which played a kind of music apparently called hard-core, which made his parents cringe.

A talented artist, as a kid he used to draw cartoon figures, like Joe the Toucan and Sheldon the Turtle. Sometimes called a gentle giant, he also like origami and many things Japanese. Anthony had a big heart. As a three-year-old at Montessori school, his dad was startled one day when he was thanked by the parent of a classmate, a special-needs child. Anthony, it turns out, was his only playmate. Nor did he like passing a panhandler without tossing a coin or two in, said his mother; the indifference upset him.

He was a popular student at D'Arcy McGee High School before starting a two-year visual arts program at Heritage College. As a teenager, he liked making short movies with his buds and, at times, wondered about a career in film.

His parents were at a cottage when the accident occurred. Daughter Alanna, 15, reached her mother on her cell. It was bad, but how bad? They didn't know.

When they arrived at the Hull hospital, the couple actually bumped into members of the Crawford family, who waited in equally grim anticipation.

They passed a room that said Salle de Pathologie. The door was ajar; David saw two gurneys, with sheets over faces. It began to sink in.

A nurse held Monica's hand. When the doctor spoke, she could hardly breathe. Against advice, she had to see her boy. She had nursed him and read to him, and walked him to the park, raised him; loved him the way only mothers can.

And it was down to this. His face was grayish, he looked asleep, with only a little blood visible, his eyes a tiny bit open. She touched him, she said, and spoke to him for a while. "My baby," she said in her kitchen; a sob said the rest.

Days later, she was speaking to her parish priest about the likely name of the foundation, Tony's Promise, and they remarked on how it can read two ways: the promise young people make in his name; the promise he can never personally fulfill.

"What was all that careful bringing-up about?"

Well, who can know? To bring them to this point, one supposes; to allow Tony's Promise to live.

Alanna wants to be involved. And she knows why. "I do it because I want the world to know how great a brother he was, in every single way."

Anthony Joseph McColl will be waked on Easter Sunday and laid to rest Easter Monday, led into St. Mark the Evangelist by a bagpiper. His mates want to sing a well known song, Monica reports, and you will know its title and tune, its words, its mourn: Amazing Grace."

To contact Kelly Egan, please call 613-726-5896, or e-mail

kegan@ottawacitizen.com

2. "The End", MacLean's Magazine, May 9, 2011

By: Stephanie Findlay

"Anthony Joseph McColl was born in Gatineau, Que., on March 11, 1992, the first of two children to David, a manager at an Ottawa travel agency, and Monica Thibault, a social worker at an Ottawa health centre. He quickly stood out for his strength. Still in the hospital—he was being monitored in an incubator for fear of being diagnosed with diabetes like his mother—his father was doing his first diaper change when the newborn grabbed hold of the metal rail. "He just managed to grab hold of it and he was about to pull himself off the change table," says Dave. "He was incredibly strong."

With big cheeks, a mop of strawberry-blond cherub curls and a boisterous spirit, toddler Anthony was energetic, physical and gregarious. His family nickname, Ant, was incongruous with his bigness. "People would say, 'Why isn't he talking?' " says Monica, who says strangers would peg him at seven or eight. "Sorry to disappoint you," she'd say, "but he's three." In 1995, sister Alanna was born. "He would rub my tummy and talk to her," says Monica. "He wanted to help me give her first bath."

Exposed to art by his family (his father was an avid photographer), Anthony became interested in things Japanese, drawing from Miyazaki films and characters from Yu-Gi-Oh! and Pokémon. His interest in the arts would span from music—he became a vocalist in a screamo band—to video. In his early teens, without any formal training, he and three of his closest friends began work on Bow chicka wow! © Productions. The 15-year-olds would use the camera Anthony's parents lent him to "film and make dumb jokes," says Nicolas Moncion, one of the friends. "It was his camera so he was the one doing the edits—that showed a lot of his leadership skills. The video turned out great."

The inaugural episode of the series opened with Anthony—Tony, as he was called by his friends—wearing a white hat and aviator sunglasses, introducing himself as "Capital-A." Speaking in front of forested suburban homes, he launched into a polemic about emo kids. "I think it'd be a lot easier to have sex than try and deal with your emotions," he said. That episode alone has had 3,616 views on YouTube; in total over 10,000 people watched Bow chika wow!© TV.

One of the more active of his friends, Anthony participated in extracurriculars at D'Arcy McGee, his high school. He played football and rugby, and starred in school plays, including a turn as Nathan Detroit in *Guys and Dolls*. As a B student, Anthony didn't stand out academically, but he shone socially. *"It was a sense of security—if you're with Anthony you feel safe and accepted,"* says friend Jonathan Carroll. Such trustworthiness prompted descriptions of Anthony as a "big teddy bear" and close confidant. He was most devoted, however, to his younger sister Alanna. Talking about her was taboo in his circle of friends: he didn't want to hear any cracks from the guys about hooking up with her.

Eager for independence, Anthony got his drivers' license soon after his 16th birthday. He took a delivery job at Dinty Moore's Restaurant—"Dinty's"—a pizza and Greek restaurant in Aylmer. On a typical night, he'd do his deliveries until 8 p.m., then come home for a barbecue dinner before heading out with his friends. He was a connoisseur of a good bonfire, Viceroy cigarettes and 10 per cent beer. He took the route of his friends and went to Heritage College, the Anglophone CEGEP in the Outaouais. Unsurprisingly, he studied visual arts.

Yet, nearing the final semesters, Anthony was getting restless. After Friday's class one early spring day, he met with friends at a Tim Horton's and told them he had just completed a forest firefighter training course and was looking for a summer placement. The conversation drifted to parties; Anthony mentioned one that Alanna, 15, was intending to go to that Friday night. His friends were uninterested, but Anthony wanted to make sure she'd be safe and made the half-hour drive anyway.

Around 2:30 a.m., Saturday April 16, it was time for the McColls to go home. Alanna asked her brother for a lift, but he already had four girls in his car and so gave her $20 for a cab instead. Alanna left first; driving east, her cab passed by an erratic westbound car pursued by police on Highway 148. Anthony, who was driving minutes behind his sister, was unable to swerve out of the way and the two cars hit head-on. Both the driver and Anthony were killed instantly. Anthony was 19."

3. Jessa's Dream

"About four months after the accident, I had a dream about
Tony. I wrote it down in my sketchbook, right after I woke up,
so that I wouldn't forget the details. I figured I'd write it all
down, beginning to end, and that way, the people involved
would get a chance to know what it was like.
I suppose it took place about 5 years or so, after we graduated.
I was a cleaning lady for an apartment building I think, and so
I had the keys to all the rooms, etc. The apartment building had
a huge tree growing in the middle of it, a pine tree I believe,
and I was going to the top floor where the top of the tree would
be. It clearly had been a while since I'd seen anyone from high
school or college, so when I walked into the apartment, I was
really surprised (And extremely happy) to see Tony, standing
there in the kitchen.
"Hey! How's it going?!"
Only Tony wasn't so crazy about seeing me. Not like he used to
be... and I mean, even if he wasn't really "excited" to see me, he
would still give me a smile, a big bear hug (which I miss
terribly) or at least a "Oh hey Jessaaaa, how's it gooooiiiin'?"
He was different this time; Quiet, shy, even though he had
recognized me. He had changed. And this is what was most
emotional for me, because I was hoping that the one time I
WOULD see him in my dreams; that he would at least smile for

me. It was almost like he was avoiding something, he would barely look at me.

We didn't REALLY talk much (that I can remember...) but I had noticed on his kitchen table that there were intensely creative and talented drawings of people we knew. Unfortunately I don't remember who they were, but I know they were our friends. So when I asked him how things were, he told me he was living with a good friend of ours, Jonathan Carroll, which didn't come to much of a surprise, but I was happy. Tony told me Jonathan was in his bedroom, so I went to see him.

Jonathan was in the same sort of state, while sitting on his bed, he wasn't really looking at me, and wasn't terribly happy to see me. I asked him how he was doing, and told him that I thought it was great he was living with Tony! Then he looked at me, with a puzzled look on his face.

I said, "You know, Anthony? Your best friend?" And he just continued to look at me with a look of dismay on his face, and he told me. "Jessa, I thought you had heard that Tony died 5 years ago in a car crash."

So what... had I hallucinated him? Did I see his ghost? Why did he look so sad? The questions kept coming...

And this is where I nearly died... (In the dream, I mean) My knees buckled and I fell to the ground crying, actually, quite similar to the reaction I had when I first heard the news. I *could not believe it. In reality, that feeling started to fade after time, the feeling of that hole being ripped into your heart, but when I woke after this, it was there all over again, and the rest of my day was a painful one.*

A couple of weeks later, my boyfriend and I were looking at a dream dictionary by chance, and I immediately thought of the one I had of Tony, and so I looked up a few things that were in the dream, and what I learned actually made quite a bit of sense. First of all, I looked at what it meant to see people who had passed, and it says that usually, they have a message for you, but this didn't quite make sense, because we barely talked – but then I thought of his drawings. Maybe he was trying to tell me that he still thinks of all of us, and always will, and that he loves us. And finally, I thought of the tree in the apartment: what could that have to do with anything? Well, trees are symbols of life, and trees that are green year round (like a pine) are signs of eternal life, because they never really die. This hit a nerve. I had never really been into all this dream stuff, never really believed that they could mean something from time to time. But this? This dream meant everything. THAT was his message -that even though he's not here in body, his life is eternal, and that he lives in all of us."
With Love,
-Jessa Leduc

4. Laurie Wilson, "The Accidental Medium"

Anthony's Message.

"Mommy!!! Wake up! Wake Up!" Chloe is sitting straight up in bed in the darkened room. She's got both hands on my bare left arm, yanking me from a deep sleep. We're supposed to be in the middle of a sleepover at Mom's condo. Chloe and I are bunking in Mom's room. We all went to bed late. It's well past midnight, the exact time unsure. This is too soon to wake up.

I'm barely conscious. "what's the matter, Chlo?" I murmur.

Chloe is talking in a stage whisper. "Mommy. I'm scared... There's somebody here. They're here on my side. I don't know who it is. Can we change sides? Please? I'm scared..."

"o.k.", I sigh as I slide towards her, pull her up and over me and settle her on the other side of the bed. I scoot over to Chloe's well-warmed spot. I find her soft white blankie and her dog-eared bunny toy nestled there. I snuggle them down beside Chloe who is now almost back to sleep, then I roll over on my side to get more shuteye.

But I can't. There's definitely somebody here. I stop trying to sleep and try to discern the subtle but pressing energy. It feels like a male presence. It's moving around this corner of the room. A paper rustles, something softly scuffs a surface. He's by the bed again – it's a calm gentle energy. It could be my Dad, or my grandfather or ...? The usual suspects would normally let me know exactly who they are. And there are a few others who tend to wake us up at night. Who is it?

But it's weird. Nighttime visitations have never happened at Mom's condo. Whoever it is, is not making himself known. I know I'll find out soon enough if it's important. I try again to settle down to sleep.

I can't. I wonder what he needs?

Sunlight is leaking around the edges of the drapes when Maya and Mom tiptoe into the room. Chloe is snoring softly on her side of the bed as I whisper to Mom that Chloe didn't sleep well. We need to let her sleep in. Someone woke her up. Someone has definitely been in the room. It felt like it was a male. Mom whispers she's not slept well either. Maya was very restless, flopping around like a fish out of water. We both agree. Something's "up".

Bleary-eyed with coffee in hand, Mom and I try to revive ourselves in the living room. As I gradually perk up I think more about last night. Very strange. Chloe would normally tell me to get rid of the unknown visitor – tell them to go away. People she doesn't know she calls "monsters" – I guess that because she's scared, they don't come in clearly enough to be seen. I'd say the usual: 'Thanks but no thanks. We can't help you now. Please go.' They usually do.

During these situations, Chloe always asks me to call in Grampa Grant to watch over us to make sure nobody will bug us. But last night I didn't do any of this. Did Chloe feel this person was meant to be with us? I guess I may have felt that too. At least it never occurred to me to ask them to leave. The energy was somehow familiar.

With both girls now up and busy munching on breakfast, I slip into Mom's bathroom for a quick shower. I'm not fully positioned under the showerhead when I hear the matter-of-fact statement in my head, "Someone close to you has died."

"Whaaat?" I say back, incredulous. This is awful. My mind whips into worst-case-scenario. Oh God, I hope it's not Bob. He's in the air right now on his way here, to be with his family. It's a stormy morning, with high winds.

I'm given no more details.

But when I get out of the shower, I hear the phone ring. The voice in my head says unemotionally, "Here we go..." I peek out the bathroom door and Mom is in the bedroom, portable phone to her ear, tears streaming down her face. "You better talk to Laurie" she says into the phone.

It's my brother Andy. Andy is in charge of calling people. We're his first call. He can hardly talk. Brief details. Anthony was in a fatal car accident early this morning. I get hit by a wave of grief. Anthony is such a great kid. Everybody loves Anthony. This is devastating. Oh God. Poor Rufus and Monica. As parents, it's their worst fear realized. This shouldn't be happening. It's not right.

Then a thought bubbles up. Could it be Anthony who visited last night? What time was the crash? What time did Chloe wake me up? Around 3 a.m. I'd guess. Chloe doesn't really know Anthony. She was a baby the last time he visited us at the lake. Whoever it was seemed to be attracted to her.

I'm packing up our sleepover bags. We're getting ready to load the car, then pick up Bob at the airport. A voice in my head says. "He's with his grandmother. He's crossed over. It was instant."

I don't know if this is wishful thinking or if it is a clear message. I let it rest.

Bob is home safe. He and I are now in our kitchen at the lake. We're making platters for the appetizer table at the annual fundraising event for Chloe's co-op preschool – it's happening tomorrow. We've finished filling spring rolls and now we're busily rolling vegetarian sushi. For no apparent reason I look up and stare at the stacked ovens. Why am I looking there? We're not using the ovens.

A male is standing there facing me. He's a big guy, he's young. Dark wavy hair falls in front of his face. It's not the first time I've had Spirit visitors beside my ovens. All the electricity – it's like a magnet. Spirits often use the energy that charges big appliances to come through to this side. My fridge has the same power, and the same effect.

Is that Anthony?? I'm not sure. He's faint. He comes in and out – at least it seems that way. I sigh. I don't enjoy this space – not knowing whether it's wishful thinking, my imagination or a real visit. But I've learned what to do. I push away the vision. If it goes away, it's wishful thinking. If the vision comes back again, gets stronger with more details, if we interact, it's the real deal.

We continue our sushi marathon. I look up from my sushi mat, frustrated with an inside-out roll that's not working for me, to find the young man standing by the ovens but this time with an older woman beside him. I think it's his grandmother. They aren't talking, just calmly surveying the scene. I acknowledge their presence. They disappear. I'm feeling it's Anthony but my ego needs more proof. I don't say anything to Bob.

It's late. The girls are now in bed and I'm in my upstairs bathroom – my channeling room – brushing my teeth, washing my face. A subtle presence comes in. I say, "Anthony, if this is you, I will help you get any messages to your family. I promise." There's no answer.

I don't sleep well. Neither does Bob. Maya wakes up. "Daddy!" She's had a bad dream and can't get back to sleep. Bob goes down to Maya's room to settle her down. I hear her cry out every time he tries to leave. He stays with her.

It's Chloe's turn. "Mommy!" Chloe often wakes up in the middle of the night. She gets up by herself to pee, read her picture books, chat with unseen friends, sing pre-school songs, recite newly learned rhymes. She only calls out if she's sick, she's wet the bed, she's hungry. Or, if there's a visitor.

I stumble down the stairs. "Mommy!" Chloe is crying now as I walk into her room. "There's somebody here!" Chloe pleads.

"It's okay, Honey. It's okay. It's just Anthony. He's our friend. He's visiting. He's a good guy. We love Anthony. Time to go back to sleep, we've got a big day tomorrow."

Chloe seems reassured. "o.k... Can you stay with me 'til when the sun comes?" Chloe mumbles from under the covers.

I agree, crawling into the spare bed. I dream that Dad is standing by my bed. He tells me in my sleep, "Anthony and Chloe have the same kind of energy."

In the morning we are scrambling to get ready for church. I'm back in my bathroom, finished my hair and now doing my face. Dad is in his usual spot, leaning against the counter, arms crossed.

"Dad? Why Anthony?"

Dad answers back immediately, "Soon you'll understand."

I reach into my walk-in closet and dig out some pant stockings from a drawer.

Dad adds, "You'll say his name in church today."

ugghh. I know what this is. It's a test from Spirit. Dad knows I like to lie low in the pew. I go to church, but as an outlier in the protestant religion, I feel it's not my place to speak up in church: I feel I'm in no position since I don't subscribe to some of its fundamental tenets. Case in point: I have not accepted Jesus Christ as my personal savior, yet this is a cornerstone of our religion.

Don't get me wrong. I'm a firm believer in what Jesus stood for, his lessons, his compassionate role model, and I am in awe of Christ consciousness that manifests every day, in warm gestures, in respectful responses, in thoughtful deeds, showing how we are all connected. The Dalai Lama sums up Christ consciousness by saying, "My religion is kindness". I subscribe to that. So I go to church.

Dad's request refers to a quiet portion during the service where churchgoers are encouraged to speak the names of people who are in their thoughts this week. Gisele, our Minister, then leads the congregation through a spontaneous community prayer that includes the names of these people. It's an unrehearsed moment where everyone seems to connect.

I make a feeble attempt to lessen my potential involvement at church this morning. "Dad, You know I don't DO that..."

Dad looks at me and waits.

"But...,"I'm thinking out loud. "I guess if there was a time to speak up, it would be today, after what happened."

"Don't worry about it, Putty," encourages Dad in my left ear. "It will all work out."

I don't know how this is going to play out. Maybe I will say something. Maybe I won't need to. I have to wait and see.

As we arrive at the front entrance to the church, I remember it's Palm Sunday. And I didn't realize there are baptisms slated for this morning. The church is packed. Lots of kids. Standing room only. Many families and friends are gathered here from our village, in from the surrounding rural countryside and up from the big city to celebrate new life and the future ahead for these beautiful newborns. They represent hope and promise for all of us.

I enjoy the ritual of the church service, the quiet hour that gives us permission to be present, the sense of community it brings out. Our Minister, Gisele, has become a good family friend. She knows about our active household, and is an insightful observer as Chloe, Maya and I – the Indigo Girls – have our adventures in Spirit.

Gisele doesn't doubt our experiences. We've sat together many times over tea to try and figure them out – look at the messages, discuss the lessons. I've often wondered how Gisele reconciles her knowledge of us with what the church teaches. Gisele grew up Catholic, but became a United Church Minister and now regularly attends Buddhist retreats. She's open, non-judgmental.

I remember last year at this time, it was Easter Sunday Communion Service. Gisele was in the pulpit. As she surveyed the congregation she had iterated another one of the church tenets "We come into this world alone, we leave this world alone." Her gaze had fallen on Bob and I. We'd gazed back at her, both of us smiling.

I personally don't believe we come into this world alone or leave it alone. We are never alone - before we come into this world, on our life's journey or as we depart. We are infinitely supported on our path by loved ones and loving beings. I see this. I KNOW this. This is my experience.

I'd already nudged Bob, muttering mischievously in his ear "Yeah. Right. That really happens." Bob had kept looking forward to the pulpit, nodding with a chuckle, while squeezing my hand.

As we left the church service that day a year ago, we give Gisele a big hug at the front entrance. Gisele is shaking her head, laughing at the inside joke. "And as I finish with 'We leave this world alone' I see the two of you smiling back at me. I'm thinking, 'WHAT am I SAYING???' I know YOU two don't believe ANY of this! How could you possibly?"

Fast forward to the present day. Today's service is longer than usual. We've got four little beings to welcome into the community. No time for a sermon. Will there be time for a community prayer? The beautiful babies are blessed and paraded around the church. Gisele finishes the baptism ritual and then asks the congregation if anyone would like to include someone in the community prayer. I surprise myself. I start speaking.

"The family of Anthony McColl", I call out without hesitation.

Gisele asks me from the front of the church, "Laurie, can you repeat Anthony's last name?"

"McColl. Anthony is only 19. He was killed by an impaired driver on Friday night."

There is a palpable hush in the congregation. I've just reminded every parent of their worst nightmare. New beginnings joyfully commemorated here are abruptly juxtaposed with a too sudden ending. I now know why I was tested this morning – told to speak up. To remind all of us gathered. Life is fragile. Hug your children. Celebrate every day.

We grab a quick bite in the village then head home to pack up appetizer trays for the next event. I'm hustling. The spring rolls need to be fried. They've turned rubbery overnighting in the fridge and must be revived. Everything is finally plated and garnished. I rush upstairs to pee, and put on some lipstick.

I'm fixing my hair. Dad's there in his usual spot. He says, "Good Job, Honey. Dad's not talking about the completed plates of sushi. It's about my speaking up in church. Dad adds, simply, "Anthony is a 5".

I stop in mid brush stroke. "Oh My God. This makes sense!"

Here's the thing. Three days before Anthony's death I've had a session with friends who are energy workers. I know my hip problem is really "issue in the tissue". I wanted to dig deeper into those unhelpful beliefs before my surgeon digs deep into my hip, so I'd set up a session with my friends Rita and Thomas.

As part of the session, Thomas, who is a medical intuitive, had asked me, "Would you like to know where you are on your soul's progression?"

My immediate gut response was, "Well, not as much as I want to deal with the issues going on now in this life. To be honest, I want to pull out the subconscious beliefs that are causing my hips to disintegrate. But I guess it would be interesting to understand where I am in the scheme of things – although I don't think it matters. You are where you are, right?"

Thomas laughed. "Well, that's right. But I can give you a quick overview of it if you like."

I agreed to the synopsis.

Thomas continued. "There is a channeled system that helps you understand why things are the way they are. It's a system that helps you see where you are on your Soul's Progression. It talks about the Soul's Path – and the system is based on a range from 1 to 5. The 1's are basically soul babies. They are naïve, have so much to learn. Fives are old souls. They've chosen to come back, they don't need to be here. Their job is simple: To enjoy the physical world in all its manifestations, and shine their light by being their true selves. They are really here to activate souls in the other ranges: their light helps to uncover hidden divine gifts and uncover buried parts of the authentic self in those souls they touch during their lifetime. In a way, it's a bit of a joy ride being a 5 – both literally and figuratively.

"Well, now I know", I said half-jokingly. "I'm definitely not an old soul! I'm coming back because I have to!"

Thomas laughed. "Well, you're a mature soul."

I'm fine with that. This soul's path was interesting info but it didn't seem relevant to me at the time. It's like being the youngest sibling, or having green eyes. I didn't "do" anything. It just is.

But now it makes sense. Anthony is a 5. I know why I was supposed to hear what Thomas had to say about the subject. I needed that piece of the puzzle to understand Anthony's divine role in this lifetime. Anthony was here to activate, to shine his light.

Dad continues, "Just look at Anthony's life."

I don't know Anthony that well but we called him "The Gentle Giant". He didn't seem afraid to embrace life, and he did it in so many ways. Rugby, art, music, laughter, hugs. He was kind, responsible, non-judgmental. He made it clear he loved his family, he loved his friends. He was true to himself, he focused on what he loved, and he made people feel good about themselves. How many souls has he activated in his lifetime? The outpouring of grief over his passing has rippled out in waves. His story is touching possibly thousands of people who never knew him. It's truly awe-inspiring.

Dad nudges me, "This is what I've been telling you, Putty. Your brain, your intellect, is important, but it's overrated. Get into your physical body. Feel its intelligence. Listen to its messages – It will tell you what you are meant to do and not. Trust its guidance and you won't get stuck on your path. You are meant to laugh, have fun, make love, dance, create! And stop! Take more time to do nothing. Just allow yourself to receive. Go out and smell your cedar trees. Listen to your birds. Feel the breeze on your face. Get out of your head, Honey. Follow your heart. Enjoy this physical life, in all its manifestations. You know this."

I nod. I know this. But I've been holding back. We live in a left brain world. Adhering to the tenets of popular culture is greatly rewarded. A book learning education holds the highest value. Busyness gets a badge of honor. Tapping into your unique inner knowledge? Swimming against the society current to follow your soul's inspiration? Not so much.

I'm a strong swimmer. In spite of my hips. It's time to trust myself, and swim upstream.

Dad says, "Chloe is a 5, too."

I have a momentary shiver. Of course. That's why Anthony would go to her first. I wonder if that means she's going to check out of this earthly plane early too? She's already had two critical scrapes, the first she turned blue and couldn't breathe, the second, her heart stopped. She's only four.

Dad is reading my mind. "Love your children, honey. The mess doesn't matter in the long run. Creating memories does." His words are reassuring. I get the distinct feeling Chloe won't even consider taking off to the higher planes until she makes a big impact in this world. Like Anthony.

When I come downstairs, Bob is already loading kids and platters into the car. It's a rainy day. I buckle up, still mulling over what Dad said upstairs. As we drive down the highway, I talk to Anthony in my head. "If it's really you Anthony, I need a sign. A distinct sign."

Bob is talking about the "to do list". It's never ending. He's gone so much of the time. It's hard to split household duties. He's taking care of the business, so I take care of the rest – the kids, the cars, the accounts, the events, the schools lunches, the bus runs, the homework, and managing the house and the home office fall to me. When Bob's away, we talk twice, maybe three times a day on the phone. Since the girls don't always sleep well at night, I get exhausted and quickly fall into overwhelm. I rely on him to help me focus on our priorities.

Bob talks above the radio music in the car. He wants to know how my work is going. He's my biggest supporter. He wants me to block out more time to develop my new online business

education program. He knows I have a lot to offer. I'm
thinking about what Dad just said.: It's time to step into my life,
get out of my head, make my dreams happen. Bob's saying the
same thing. It's time to shine my light on my business.

It's hard to shift. I'm thinking of all the things I'm responsible
for. So many trails of unfinished business. I clean up a lot of
messes. So many loose ends to be tied. Another loose end
dawns on me. I haven't bought any gifts for the teachers for
year end. I'm headed for hip surgery in four days – I won't be
shopping for a while.

"What are we going to give Deb?" I question Bob for ideas.

Deb has been Maya's and now Chloe's teacher. She's greatly
loved. Deb should be paid much more for her work. But she
loves what she does. It's not just about the money. She's truly
dedicated, passionate about child development, and committed
to the wellbeing of her flock. And the kids adore her right back.
Whatever gift we give her has to be special. Deb is part of
Maya and Chloe's extended family.

We're at the Silent Auction, chatting with parents, while the
kids play in the corners. There are lots of items to bid on. We
don't need anything. I tell my group of friends, "There are

some lovely pieces of art here, but we don't have any walls to put them on. I hope you can bid on them."

My friends are pointing out their favorite pieces when a parent organizer comes up. "Ladies, you need to buy raffle tickets to win the oil painting of the school."

I didn't notice we'd been standing right beside the raffle prize. It's a brightly colored primitive oil painting of the little red brick schoolhouse, including kids and playground. It's very sweet. I don't have a wall to put it on. But I buy a pack of five tickets for $5 to support the cause.

The other ladies are excited about this painting. It's special. It captures the wonder of our co-op pre-school. I wish I had gone to this school when I was little. I think a lot of parents wish the same thing. Lots of tickets are being sold.

As I stand there holding my tickets, a voice whispers in my ear. "You are going to win this." The tone is very matter-of-fact. It continues, "But you need to buy another set of tickets."

"Whaatt?" I say in my head. But I feel it's true. I've never felt so sure of winning something in my life. I know I'm going to win this raffle. I feel the nudge.

I call over to Bob who's talking with another Dad, "Bob, go buy another set of tickets, please." He waves at me from across the room.

I'm now talking to my close friend Carol. She's insightful, very intuitive. She's a sister from another life. She's already heard about the crash. Her husband's friend's son is a friend of Anthony. The young man is devastated by this news. We're all shaken. It's a parent's worst dream come true. And it's unthinkable for a teenager to lose a friend.

I tell Carol about the Soul System, that Anthony is an old soul. Dad says he's a 5. That he didn't have to come back. That he came back for a reason – to activate the souls here. She nods. She has already gotten the message on Face Book that Anthony's accident has touched hundreds. And it only happened 36 hours ago. Hard to believe.

Carol says, "I bet Chloe is a 5 too. "

I haven't told Carol about what's been going on in the house. About Chloe waking up the night of the crash. That Anthony seems to be visiting us and hanging out with Chloe. I'm not sure, after all. It seems too much to hope for. I need more proof.

One hour later, the raffle organizer is yelling, "Last call for tickets! Last call for tickets!" It pops into my head that Bob hasn't bought those tickets. I grab his arm, "Bob, did you buy those tickets?" He rushes over and buys another set of five tickets before the raffle sales closes.

Chloe's little friend walks up to the big jar to pull a ticket. I whisper in Bob's ear. "We're going to win this. Get your tickets out".

The organizer calls, "The Winner is...... !" She calls out the number.

Bob looks down at his ticket. Then walks over to the Raffle organizer and exclaims, "We've got the ticket!" He comes back with the primitive oil painting of our little red brick schoolhouse – and hands it to me.

He looks at me, shaking his head, incredulous. I smile back at him: "I told you we were going to win this."

"What are we going to do with this? We have no walls!" Bob is happy to win something, but he's also a practical man.

"We'll find a good home for it." I reply.

Deb comes up to us. "I'm so happy you won this. I know you'll enjoy it. And the girls will enjoy it too." She adds quietly, "I'm just a little bit sad. I bought 4 sets of tickets. I even had a spot picked out."

I thank Deb and give her a hug. I know what we're going to give her for an end-of-year teacher gift. We won it for her. It's going to be the perfect gift.

As we're getting into the car, I tell Bob we're giving the painting to Deb. Then it dawns on me. "What was the number on the ticket?"

Bob can't remember. He pulls the ticket from his pocket. "It's 0-5-0."

"Oh, My God, Bob. Anthony helped us win that raffle. He's a 5!!! He helped us get the painting. And he solved our gift idea for Deb!"

On the way home, I explain the Soul System to Bob. I tell him how Anthony has been coming in since Friday night. How he's been hanging out with Chloe. That I'd asked for distinct proof it was Anthony.

Bob doesn't question this. He feels it's Anthony. Bob says matter-of-fact, "It's the kind of thing he'd do, isn't it? Let us know he's here – with something fun, that helps people. It's very creative, how he did it."

I agree. It's exactly the kind of thing Anthony would do.

Bob is now parking the car in our driveway. "Looks like you have a job to do: Talk to Rufus and Monica. Let them know he's around."

That night we finally get the girls fed and to bed. They're having difficulty settling down. So much excitement playing with their friends at the Auction. Bob leaves the newspaper on the kitchen table – Anthony's life is outlined in a big city newspaper article. I check FaceBook. More comments. Kids are shocked. There are many posts about promising not to drink and drive, and not let friends do it either. The "promise" is spreading fast.

My sister-in-law calls me. Sheryl says, "Lo, we spent the day with them. It was so sad. I think it would really help if you called Rufus & Monica. You won't bother them."

I know. I must call. I'm not sure how that's going to play out though. Rufus and Monica don't know much about me, about our mediumship abilities. I let that thought go. What's supposed to happen will happen. I'm tired. I need to go to bed.

"Mommy!!!!!!" It's 3 am. It's Chloe.

I'm quick to Chloe's room, making sure her yells don't wake up Maya in the other room. Anthony's by the bed.

"It's okay Chloe. Anthony's here. He's our friend, remember?. I'll stay with you."

Chloe rolls over, pulls the covers over her head. I slip under the comforter on the spare bed. Soon I hear the snuffling of Chloe's soft snores. I shuffle bleary-eyed back to my room. Anthony is soon sitting on my bedside. He's very clear. He's definitely crossed over. We chat.

"Anthony. I told you that I'd tell your Mom and Dad you're here. Tell me what happened".

I hear Anthony's voice in my head., "It happened so fast." (In my head, he shows me a car coming across the centerline).

"I wasn't scared. I just tried to get out of the way. When it hit, I didn't feel anything." (I don't feel any pain in my own body as Anthony says this. I often feel the physical pain of others.)

"I just felt my body tingle – it felt good - and then I lifted up out of my body. I saw..." (Anthony shows me his grandmother looking at him through the windshield). *"She gave me a hug. She took my hand. I was so happy to see her. She's really 'alive', you know. She's here, you know."*

I know. I say, "Anthony, was this an 'accident' or was this your time?"

"Well...., if it was an accident, it was a pretty good time to go."

I understand what he's saying. It's what I've been told. He's an old soul. As we move into higher consciousness, Anthony is activating a huge number of teenagers. And many of us adults. Life is short! He's reminding us to live full out, follow our passions. But do it with care and kindness for those around us.

The next day I have errands in the city. Anthony seems to be enjoying the ride in the passenger seat. "I have friends who will want some things of mine. Tell Mom. She'll know what to give. But when the time is right. There's no rush."

He shows me a red car. It's in his room. I can't tell from the images if it's a toy car, a picture, or what. But the message is a red car. I need to tell Rufus and Monica. They'll know what it means.

I've been crossing to do's off my list and now sit in the car in the Shopper's Drugmart parking lot. The radio is on. I crank up the music. I'm nervous. I know I must call Anthony's parents. The news cuts in. There's a clip about the crash. It gives me the nudge. I pick up my cell phone. Anthony is happy. He says, "Don't worry. You won't reach them. They're busy."

I ring the home number anyway. A woman answers. Rufus and Monica are being interviewed by a television crew. Can I call back later? I'm amazed at the media coverage this is getting.

But I also have that sinking feeling, after you crank yourself to do something difficult, only to find you have to wait it out. Anthony has this grin on his face. "I told you!"

I'm wondering again, how is this going to play out. The radio music filters into my brain. It's Kelly Jones singing Maybe Tomorrow. The Stereophonics' lyrics say a lot about how to live life fully, even though things may seem black at the time. And the song's refrain is "Maybe tomorrow... I'll find my way home..."

http://www.youtube.com/watch?v=d4I5kmp-rns&feature=related

Anthony says, "See? You'll talk to Mom and Dad tomorrow!"

I have to laugh. Spirit often, I mean OFTEN, uses music to get its messages across. That's one way we can tap into our loved ones who've left this physical plane. When you are thinking of them, turn on your favorite radio station and listen to the music.

Anthony changes the subject. He confesses, "I've been kinda bugging Alanna."

Once a big brother, always a big brother.

"What are you doing to that poor girl?" I admonish.

"I've been... kinda teasing her. Pulling her hair. Things are dropping for no reason."

I see a pencil rolling off a desk, a book falls out of a girl's hand; Alanna is swiping stray hairs away from her face.

"Does she know it's you?" I ask.

"I think she does but she's afraid to believe it."

"She's afraid?" I'm saying this with just a bit of pointed parental irritation.

"I know..."Anthony admits he's possibly freaking out his sister. "I'm backin' off..."

"I'll get the message to her that it's you. Just don't stand so close. 'K?"

"Thank youuuuu." he replies in a monotone.

Sheryl calls me that night. "Did you see the CTV interview with Monica and Rufus? It's posted on the CTV website."

I fire up the computer. Rufus and Monica are sitting close to each other at their kitchen table, talking to the reporter about the accident, about the parents of the son who plowed into Anthony's vehicle.

Rufus has tears in his eyes. He's saying, "We hold no judgment. This could have happened to any of us. We've all lost a child in this tragedy". Monica is nodding her head in agreement.

At this moment, I start to cry. I am so proud of those two. It's an honor to be a friend of theirs. Their compassion and forgiveness is truly remarkable. They are role models for us all. They didn't follow the typical "easy" path of blame. They rose above it.

I see movement out of the corner of my eye. I look up from my dining room table. Anthony is coming through. He's got his arm around someone's shoulders. It's another young man. I cannot see the man's face - It's blurry. And his energy feels unsure, nervous, possibly a little frightened. The young man doesn't speak.

Anthony looks me straight in the eye and states, "We're not leaving him behind."

That's when it hits me. It's the boy who crashed into Anthony. But he's lost. He's not crossed over. Anthony is staying with him. Reassuring him. This is what Anthony would do in this life.

Before they fade away, Anthony adds, "Look at the video again – I'm with them. I'm standing behind Mom, on her left side."

I go back to the computer, and press 'play' on the CTV news video. I scan the scene for signs. I don't see Anthony. But I do see Monica is wearing a crisp white shirt - and there's a spot on her left shoulder that is surprisingly crinkled, where a hand might rest.

As I listen again to Rufus's words of forgiveness, I am struck by the true meaning of Anthony's words...'We're not leaving him behind'. Anthony is telling us he's working through the veil, co-creating with his parents. They are a team. That family will always be a team. By voicing their compassion, Rufus and Monica will help the young man release from this earth. He won't get stuck here, attached to the physical realm. He'll be freed.

And Anthony's family's words and actions will encourage others to forgo judgment. What's done is done. No need to create more pain by criticizing, finding fault, laying blame. This tragedy could have happened to anyone. How we choose to respond to the heartbreak is what counts. It's about choosing kindness and forgiveness and compassion. It's about choosing love. That's Anthony's message."

Photos

His first year.

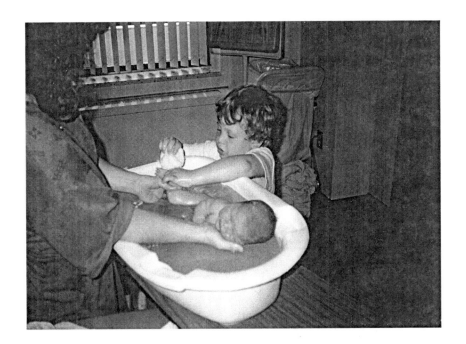

His relationship with his sister was strong right from the beginning. Here, Anthony helps give Alanna her first bath. She was thirteen hours old.

A fun portrait.

With Ms. Holland, his grade six teacher.

Hoisting his sister Alanna, after she scored her first try in her very first rugby game.

Big tackles in high school, 2009.

With mom on his 18th birthday. March 11, 2010.

He pretended not to like this.

Christmas, 2008 (with Casper the cat)

It wasn't just my wife and I that noticed how close a relationship Anthony had with his sister. Their friends could see the strong bond between the two of them as well. We held a Sweet Sixteen party on Alanna's 16th birthday, four months after the crash. This piece of art was painted by Alanna's good friend Renee Langlois and given to Alanna at the party. Incidentally, the shirt Anthony is wearing in the photo was his favorite shirt and he was wearing it the night he died. We manage to get it back from the hospital.

A very high impact crash. It is almost impossible to see the driver's door.

The roadside memorial. The provincial authorities have decided that because there are so many roadside memorials on Highway 148 (the highway of tears) they are a distraction to drivers. They have removed all memorials from the side of the highway including my son's.

His pallbearers were some of his best friends. Easter
Monday, April 24, 2011.

Photo: Gilles Desbiens, The Aylmer Bulletin

At the far left is Parker Johnston. At the far right is Richard Beard, they are two of the four great young men who created Tony's Promise. They were close friends of Anthony and his sister Alanna. The people in the middle are the first responders who rushed to the crash scene that night. The two Fire Fighters in the foreground are holding the actual Jaws of Life that were used to cut the girls out of Anthony's vehicle. It took them a full hour to get all of the girls out of the car.

The Fire Fighters from left to right are; Denis Martineau, Evan Prest, Francis Madore, Cheryl Hardwick, Dan Groleau, Michelle Dubois and Marcel Martineau. Each and every one of them are heroes.

Thank You

I want to thank the following individuals and organizations for supporting me, my family and the Tony's Promise campaign.

The great men and women of the Luskville Fire Department.

Breathalyzer Canada and Lifeloc Technologies

http://www.breathalyzercanada.com

P.A.R.T.Y.

Prevent Alcohol and Risk Related Trauma in Youth

http://www.ottawahospital.on.ca/wps/portal/Base/TheHospital/ClinicalServices/DeptPgrmCS/Programs/PARTY

Richard Beard, Andy Guest, Parker Johnston and Luc Leblanc (The Fantastic Four), for creating the Tony's Promise campaign and helping in every possible way.

Rick and Peggy Henderson, I love you both.

Principal George Singfield and the staff and students of; D'Arcy McGee High School, Symmes Junior High School Philemon Wright High School.

Thank you, cont'd

The Aylmer Community Theatre Company (ACTCo)
http://www.actcompany.ca/

Every member of the Tony's Promise FaceBook group.

The community of Aylmer, Quebec.

Everyone who supported my family and me throughout this ordeal.

The Forum Sports Bar in Gatineau, Quebec.

Martin Crosbie, Author of the best selling novel, "My Temporary Life".

Kate Burns for designing the Tony's Promise logo and helping me with the cover of this book. She's also a great writer. Check out her book at the following link:

http://www.amazon.com/The-Ophelia-Trap-Kate-Burns/dp/1604819170/ref=sr_tc_2_1?ie=UTF8&qid=13426
55196&sr=1-2-ent

CPSIA information can be obtained at www.ICGtesting.com
Printed in the USA
LVOW082027181112

307856LV00023B/411/P

9 781479 126514